"A STRANGER TO THE FUR TRADE"

JOSEPH WRIGLEY AND THE TRANSFORMATION OF THE HUDSON'S BAY COMPANY, 1884-1891

by **Eleanor Stardom**

Rupert's Land Research Centre
University of Winnipeg
Winnipeg, Canada R3B 2E9

1995

Eleanor Stardom
  "A Stranger to the Fur Trade": Joseph Wrigley and the Transformation of the
Hudson's Bay Company, 1884-1891.

Rupert's Land publication series.
  General editor: Jennifer S.H. Brown.

ISBN: 0-921206-25-9

CONTENTS

MAPS / TABLES

ABBREVIATIONS

CP   Caron Papers, National Archives of Canada, Ottawa
DCB   Dictionary of Canadian Biography
GI   Glenbow-Alberta Institute, Calgary
HBC   Hudson's Bay Company
HBCA   Hudson's Bay Company Archives, Provincial Archives of
          Manitoba, Winnipeg
HSM   Historical Society of Montana, Helena
MTL   Metropolitan Toronto Library
NAC   National Archives of Canada, Ottawa
NLC   National Library of Canada, Ottawa
PAM   Provincial Archives of Manitoba, Winnipeg

ACKNOWLEDGMENTS

This study is a revised version of my M.A. thesis presented to the Department of History at the University of Manitoba. Having grown up in a small Manitoba town on the resource frontier, I was naturally attracted to fur trade history during my undergraduate studies. When I began graduate work, the presence of the Hudson's Bay Company Archives in Winnipeg offered a unique opportunity to do primary research in my area of interest.

I would like to thank Arthur J. Ray, University of British Columbia and Jack Bumsted, University of Manitoba for their initial contributions. Jennifer Brown, general editor of the Rupert's Land Research Centre at the University of Winnipeg, edited the manuscript for publication with care and patience. I am indebted to Ed Rea for his critical comments and encouragement as well as his initial supervision of my thesis. Renée Fossett provided the indexing and Murray Stardom, Catharine Dunlop and Thea Stone assisted with computer graphics.

I reserve special thanks for Scott Reid, formerly of the Hudson's Bay Company Archives. Without his assistance and that of his colleague, Anne Morton, this project would never have reached completion.

Much of the material in the first chapter originally appeared in an article for *The Beaver* and is reprinted here with their permission. Randy Rostecki kindly allowed me to use a compilation of several maps from his M.A. thesis.

They all have earned my gratitude but bear no responsibility for any errors, which are mine alone.

INTRODUCTION

The post-1870 period was one of rapid change in Hudson's Bay Company history. Once it had enjoyed exclusive trade rights and legal jurisdiction across the vast expanse of Rupert's Land under the terms of the original charter of 1670. In 1869, the Deed of Surrender reduced it to the status of a private company, forced to compete in an open market under the jurisdiction of the Canadian government.

With the transfer of a major portion of its territory to the Dominion Government, the nature of the company's trading operations altered significantly. As its attention shifted northwards to the fur resources of the distant Athabaska and Mackenzie River regions, spiralling transportation costs prompted the company to streamline the entire fur trade system. More efficient routes were developed and less labour-intensive methods of inland transportation were introduced, such as which enabled the company to move heavy cargo at a fraction of previous costs. In southern regions, consolidation measures adopted in the 1820s by Governor George Simpson were stepped up. Winnipeg was designated as the major depot, reducing York Factory and Norway House to mere trading posts serving their immediate districts. On the prairies the surge of new settlers which followed the completion of the railway dramatized the potential of the company's retail trade which began to play an increasingly important role in its operations by the 1880s.

To ensure proper administration and effective control of its commercial interests, in conjunction with those of the fur trade, the company created the position of trade commissioner in 1884 to which it appointed Joseph Wrigley. His appointment broke with the company's long-standing tradition of selecting administrators for its British North American trade from among its commissioned officers who were experienced in the fur trade. Although Wrigley had an established background in commerce, having spent many years in the English textile business, he had no previous connections with the company, the fur trade or Canada.

Wrigley's seven-year term (1884-1891) was marked by several important developments. As trade commissioner, he was involved in ongoing efforts to tap rich fur resources in the Northern and Western Departments as efficiently as possible. Although the company's attention would gradually shift towards its land holdings and commercial ventures, the fur trade remained a viable part of its operations and a revenue base for diversification. The 1880s also witnessed a decline in the role of the commissioned officers, the traditional backbone of the company's fur trade operations. Their success in obtaining major concessions from the Governor and Committee in 1879, to compensate for two consecutive years without remuneration, was the high point of the post-1870 period and their importance in the company's operations declined steadily over the next decade.

In 1888, Wrigley presided over the last of the historic councils of the company's commissioned officers. Shortly after, in 1893, the company extinguished the Deed Poll of 1871 and with it the system of profit-sharing established in 1821, reducing the status of the commissioned officers to that of salaried employees.

It was the company's plan to compensate for the decline in the fur trade by expanding its retail trade under Wrigley's administration. As towns and cities sprang up in the wake of the railway, local fur trade posts often took on the role of general stores. Bartering was replaced by a credit and cash system which capitalized on treaty funds, government contracts and an expanding wage-earning society. As the number of HBC retail outlets increased, centralized storage depots were established as bases for commercial and fur trade operations in an attempt to compete more effectively with other entrepreneurs. Their aggressive competition, coupled with a widespread economic depression, were determining factors in the success of Wrigley's efforts to develop the company's retail operations.

A second aspect of the company's operations which emerged in response to increased settlement was the development of its land interests under the administration of Land Commissioner Charles J. Brydges. The selection of Winnipeg over Selkirk in 1881 as the transcontinental railway's gateway to the west, coupled with a temporary easing of world depression, stimulated land sales and resulted in a short-lived economic boom. To increase the attractiveness of its land holdings, the company expanded its network of retail outlets, and constructed grist and saw mills under Wrigley's administration.

The collapse of the boom had serious financial repercussions which forced a major reorganization of company management in 1884. Donald A. Smith, former land commissioner (1874-1879) and outspoken critic of Land Commissioner Brydges, obtained a position on the London board and was appointed, with Sandford Fleming, to a two-man advisory subcommittee to supervise the company's North American operations. All of the land and trade commissioners' correspondence was subsequently rerouted through their office creating a significant shift in the balance of power within the corporate structure.

This study examines the relationship between Trade Commissioner Wrigley, the Canadian subcommittee and the London-based Governor and Committee with particular emphasis on the role of Donald A. Smith. The London board's inability to recognize the need to separate the responsibilities of ownership from that of local management, a failure that hindered the company's development in all sectors of the trade, also receives particular attention.

The relationship between the Hudson's Bay Company and the Dominion Government was often confrontational during Wrigley's term of office but, in 1885, their objectives coincided. Wrigley played a major role in the North West Rebellion as the person responsible for the provisioning and transport of field forces travelling west. Although Wrigley was critical of the government's inept handling of Indian and Métis concerns, he recognized that the company had an important stake in supporting its efforts to suppress the uprising. The HBC's network of trading posts and transportation routes made it vulnerable to attacks which would have had disastrous consequences for its land and commercial interests. Wrigley's task was hampered by the Ottawa bureaucrats' ignorance of western Canada and by an entrenched patronage system which frustrated his attempts to establish efficient logistics. Even more important was the lack of a clearcut chain of command, a problem that later had serious financial repercussions when the company submitted its accounts to the war claims commission.

Finally, the study attempts to determine the exact circumstances surrounding Wrigley's abrupt departure from HBC service in 1891. He returned with his family to England where he remained until his death in 1926.

The majority of the general histories of the Hudson's Bay Company have focused on the pre-1870 period of the fur trade. E.E. Rich's *History of the Hudson's Bay Company, 1670-1870* provides an excellent background which is crucial to understanding the events of subsequent decades. Morris Zaslow's *The Opening of the Canadian North 1870-1914* offers a concise overview of the Hudson's Bay Company's diversified operations during this transition period. Although Zaslow touches briefly on its land and commercial interests, he emphasizes the evolution of new transportation systems and routes within the wider context of northern development. A.A. den Otter's article, "The Hudson's Bay Company's Prairie Transportation Problem 1870-85", focuses on Commissioner James A. Grahame, Wrigley's predecessor, his role in the development of water transportation and his attempts to reconcile it with railway technology. Robert V. Oleson's thesis, "The Commissioned Officers of the Hudson's Bay Company and the Deed Poll in the 1870's with Particular Emphasis on the Fur Trade Party, 1878-1879," examines the changes in the fur trade component of the company's operations and provides background for the shift to land and retail trade which occurred during the next decade. Gary Sealey's thesis, "History of the Hudson's Bay Company, 1870-1900," also studies the development of the fur trade, but because his research was then limited by the Hudson's Bay Company's restriction on its post-1870 archival material, his conclusions are based on manuscript sources, HBC publications and government documents which refer only tangentially to the company.

Several historians have focused on the growing importance of the company's land holdings during the 1880s which coincided with the development of retail trade. They include J.S. Galbraith, "Land Policies of the Hudson's Bay Company, 1870-1913"; Alan Wilson, "In A Business Way: C.J. Brydges and the Hudson's Bay Company, 1879-1889"; H. John Selwood and Evelyn Baril, "The Hudson's Bay Company and Prairie Town Development"; and Hartwell Bowsfield (ed.), *The Letters of Charles John Brydges*, 2 vols. The second volume (1883-1889) is particularly important in tracing the relationship between the newly created office of trade commissioner, the land commissioner and the London board.

Relatively little has been written on the company's initial ventures into retail trade with the exception of Henry Klassen's studies of the Hudson's Bay Company and I.G. Baker & Co. in southwestern Alberta. His article on the HBC's development from fur trade posts to general stores and small department stores traces the typical pattern of the company's evolution in settled areas of western Canada.

Most works which deal specifically with the period from 1884 to 1891 give Wrigley little more than passing mention. Two exceptions are Desmond Morton and Reginald H. Roy (eds.), *Telegrams of the North-West Campaign 1885*, and J.E. Rea's article, "The Hudson's Bay Company and the North West Rebellion." Both, however, confine their discussion of Wrigley to an assessment of his role in the events of 1885.

The recognized authority on the modern fur trade is Arthur J. Ray, whose book *The Canadian Fur Trade in the Industrial Age*, provides a detailed examination of the fur trade industry in Canada until 1945 with particular emphasis on the post World War I period.   In the preface, he acknowledges the difficulties faced by fur trade scholars of the post 1870 era.   Although company records prior to 1870 had been opened to researchers as early as 1931, it was not until 1970 that records from 1870 to 1900 were made available in the company's London archives.[1]   In 1974 these archives were transferred to the Provincial Archives of Manitoba making accessible a wealth of new information on economic and social issues critical to the study of the development of Western Canada.   Based on these resources, the significance of the role played by Joseph Wrigley in the company's transformation to a modern enterprise can now be explored.

---

[1]Arthur J. Ray, *The Canadian Fur Trade in the Industrial Age*, p. xvii.

Chapter 1

FROM EMPIRE TO ENTERPRISE

In August 1884, Joseph Wrigley arrived in Winnipeg to take up his duties as the Hudson's Bay Company's first trade commissioner, in charge of fur and general trade. Unlike his predecessors, Chief Commissioners Donald A. Smith and James A. Grahame, who had worked their way up through the ranks of the fur trade, Wrigley had no previous connection with the HBC. By breaking with tradition and choosing to look outside the organization for a man with broad commercial experience, the company embarked on the final phase of its transition from a fur trade monopoly to a diversified corporation, a process which had been evolving since 1870.

That year marked the end of a two-hundred-year era in Hudson's Bay Company history. An Order in Council, signed in London on 23 June 1870, admitting Rupert's Land and the North West Territory into the Dominion of Canada completed the transfer of authority and brought to an end two centuries of HBC rule. Effective 15 July 1870, the company was reduced from a royally chartered British monopoly, with judicial and administrative responsibilities in addition to its economic goals, to a private business operating under the regulations of Canadian law. Stripped of the privileges of monopoly, it now had to contend with more aggressive entrepreneurs, whose trading skills had been honed by competition, in an area on the brink of rapid expansion.

The terms of the transfer were straightforward. Based on the Deed of Surrender signed by Governor Sir Stafford H. Northcote on 19 November 1869 in anticipation of a transfer on 1 December, the company received £300,000 from the Canadian government in return for its landed rights. The company was entitled to retain its trading posts and to select a block of land adjoining each post within twelve months of the final surrender, the grand total not to exceed 50,000 acres. In addition, the company was permitted to select grants of land not exceeding one-twentieth of the total area from any township or district within the Fertile Belt.[2] These grants had to be claimed within ten years of a township's survey, and were restricted to the remaining unsold land.

Relieved of the burden of governing, the company was now free to concentrate on developing its resources. By November 1870, the board had commissioned an independent agent, Cyril Graham, to undertake a tour of its North American operations as the first step in an overall review of the company's organization.[3] He had three

---

[2]HBC, *Charters, Statutes, Orders in Council, etc. Relating to the Hudson's Bay Company*, p. 11. The Fertile Belt was described as the area bounded on the south by the United States boundary, on the west by the Rocky Mountains, on the north by the northern branch of the Saskatchewan River and on the east by Lake Winnipeg (ibid., p. 176).

[3]It was stressed to shareholders that Cyril Graham was not connected in any way with the Hudson's Bay Company. He had served as private secretary to Lord Carnarvon

(continued...)

objectives. First, he was to determine how the fur trade could be made more productive and economical. Second, he was to examine the formal arrangement between the company and its commissioned officers who were responsible for the management of the fur trade in the company's territories, "so as to place the latter on a footing better adapted to existing circumstances."[4] Finally, he was to investigate ways in which other branches of the company's business could be developed. The wide range of options that Governor Northcote offered for Graham's consideration indicated the degree to which the London board was willing to entertain new ideas at this critical stage of development.[5]

Recognizing that the relationship between the company's London operations and its commissioned officers was crucial to success in any sphere of business, Graham recommended that the board reconsider its opposition to the continuation of the Guarantee of 1865 which established a minimum annual income for commissioned officers to compensate for fluctuations inherent in the fur trade. The agreement expired in June of 1869, and Graham warned that rejecting a proposed extension would be regarded by the officers as little short of a breach of faith.[6] No matter how distasteful such a measure might be to the shareholders, the company could not afford to alienate experienced men. The loss of their allegiance would effectively cripple the fur trade, threaten any aspirations toward a general business and, in short, "practically ruin you". Graham also proposed the addition of two more ranks of service which would provide more opportunities for promotion and attract a better class of men.

Rejecting the traditional Lake Winnipeg route to the west as too hazardous, he recommended the introduction of steam vessels on the Saskatchewan River, Lake Winnipegosis and Lake Manitoba with a view to expanding service northwards. Such a system, being less labour-intensive, would enable the company to transport cargo at a fraction of the cost of York boat and Red River cart brigades and reduce its dependence on native boatmen and labourers.[7]

---

[3](...continued)
during his tenure as Colonial Secretary and, in this capacity, Graham had made many important contacts with the Canadian government during negotiations for Confederation. Since he had also visited Red River he was suited admirably for the task (HBC, *Proceedings at a General Court of the Governor and Company of Adventurers of England Trading into Hudson's Bay*, 22 November 1870, p. 5).

[4]HBCA, A.7/4, fo. 152, Governor Northcote to Cyril Graham, confidential, 30 October 1870.

[5]Ibid., fos. 153-155.

[6]HBCA, A.ll/100, Graham to Northcote, 15 March 1871, fo. 68a.

[7]H.A. Innis, *The Fur Trade in Canada*, p. 342 and A.J. Ray, "The Decline of Paternalism in the Hudson's Bay Company Fur Trade 1870-1945" in Rosemary Ommer, *Merchant Credit and Labour Strategies in Historical Perspective*, pp. 189-190.

The company could only benefit from taking the initiative in opening up the west and improving communications. Its public image could not be considered lightly. The Dominion government's argument that the company's territories should have been ceded without payment was supported by a majority of Canadians who believed that the final land and cash settlement would bolster what was traditionally believed to be its ongoing campaign to retard progress in the North West.[8] HBC demands for five per cent interest on the transfer settlement and subsequent rebellion losses claims were cited as further evidence of greed on the part of what was widely perceived to be an enormously wealthy company.

General business received little more than passing mention in Graham's report, reflecting both the company's priorities and the local economic climate. Graham's consultations revealed that many Canadian businessmen were surprised that the company had never taken advantage of its reputation and means to pursue an extensive business in Canada. Although Graham predicted a good future in commerce, banking appeared to be a more lucrative venture. He made preliminary enquiries on the company's behalf on the premise that if the company moved aggressively in these two areas, it might regulate the commerce of the North West.

The company's land holdings appeared to hold the most promise. HBC shareholders had grandiose expectations of vast profits to be made from land sales but Graham was more cautious. He recommended that, given the current low value of land and its generally undetermined quality, the company should welcome any buyer who would take the bulk of it at a good price. Otherwise, he advocated an intermediate policy of holding back in areas likely to attract settlers and placing a minimum price on the remainder.[9]

Opinion was divided on which direction the company should take. The commissioned officers did not share London shareholders' optimism over land prospects. On the other hand, profits for the year ending in 1870 had been the lowest in years and an actual loss was recorded in 1871.[10] Seeing little future in the fur trade and with visions of more immediate profits to be made in land sales, an independent group of shareholders tabled a report urging that the fur trade be abandoned. The London board decided, however, to reorganize both the trade and transportation systems, arguing that, despite the massive capital outlay involved, they could be made both productive and remunerative.[11]

The company had good reason to recommend such a move. It had an established reputation for trading in quality goods, expertise, large resources and almost unlimited

---

[8]Chester Martin, *The Natural Resources Question, The Historical Basis of Provincial Claims*, pp. 29-34.

[9]HBCA, A.11/100, fo. 85a, Graham to Northcote, 15 March 1871.

[10]HBC, *Report of the Governor and Committee of the Hudson's Bay Company, to be Laid Before the Shareholders*, 5 July 1870, p. 5.

[11]HBC, *Proceedings*, 28 June 1871, pp. 5-6.

credit. At the forefront of the North West's economy, it was in an enviable position to capitalize on the anticipated influx of settlers. Nothing could be done, however, without the consent of the commissioned officers.

The commissioned officers' relations with the HBC were very different from those in an ordinary company in that they were not considered employees in the normal sense. Instead of a salary they were entitled to a share of the profits based on their seniority. They had legal rights which were outlined in the Deed Poll[12] and could not be dismissed at will. Therefore their legal interests in the company had to be bought out before any administrative reorganization could be contemplated.

As a first step, a new Deed Poll was drawn up incorporating three new ranks of officers who would share in the traditional 40 per cent of the clear gains and profits from the fur and general trade. They were excluded, however, from any share of the land revenue. After prolonged and heated negotiations spanning several months, the retiring interests of the commissioned officers were finally bought out, effective 2 June 1872.[13]

Although they had successfully used the threat of mass resignation to obtain monetary demands, the commissioned officers were ultimately losers in the new agreement. With their 40 per cent of the profits subdivided into 100 shares instead of 85, as had been done formerly, each officer received a smaller share.[14] Although there were three new ranks, the total number of officers dropped from 54 to 50. The net result was fewer men with greater responsibilities. The board refused to consider any provision for a guaranteed income and assumed complete control of the retirement fund. The system of promotion by seniority, outlined in the Deed Poll of 1834, was abolished, opening the way for appointments from outside the company.

In addition, a new salaried position of chief commissioner was created. As the company's chief representative in Canada, he had direct authority over the commissioned officers and assumed all powers formerly vested in the governors and councils of the various departments. His primary responsibility was to monitor annual trade results and submit accounts to the London board. As well, he was to oversee administration of the

---

[12]The Deed Poll, first established in 1821 and revised in 1834, was a legal document which set down rules and regulations pertaining to the fur trade and the rights and responsibilities of the commissioned officers. It could not be altered without the consent of the governors and councils of the various departments.

[13]HBC, *Proceedings*, 28 June 1871, pp. 1-50 and HBC, *Proceedings*, 12 July 1871, pp. 1-60.

[14]The four inspecting chief factors received 3 shares each; eight chief factors received 2.5 shares each; twenty factors received 2 shares each; ten chief traders received 1.5 shares each and eight junior chief traders received 1 share each. The remaining five shares were applied to a fund to support retired officers and their families (HBCA, A.33/1, *Agreement between the Governor and Committee of the Hudson's Bay Company and the undersigned Chief Factors and Chief Traders appointed under the terms of the Deed Poll of June 1834*).

company's numerous trading posts and establish rules and regulations for the conduct of the trade.[15]

The man appointed by the board to this position was Donald A. Smith. A native of Scotland, he had signed on with the company as an apprentice clerk in 1838 and had spent the majority of the next 29 years in Labrador. In 1851 he was promoted to the rank of chief trader. Ten years later he became a chief factor and, in 1869, he was appointed to the charge of the Montreal Department.[16] During his final years in Labrador he embarked on an investment career, acting on behalf of many of the commissioned officers in conjunction with his cousin George Stephen, an entrepreneur and skilled investor who introduced Smith to other influential men of the period such as E.H. King, manager of the Bank of Montreal, and shipowner Hugh Allan.

Smith gained national prominence in 1870 as one of three special commissioners appointed by the Canadian government to act as mediators and investigators during the Red River uprising. After Louis Riel's escape from Red River, Smith became the chief civil authority in Rupert's Land until Lieutenant Governor Adams G. Archibald's arrival. In July of that year, the company appointed Smith president of the Council of the Northern Department and in this capacity he was entrusted by the commissioned officers to represent their claims before the London board for a share of the £300,000 transfer money from the Canadian government.

His increasing influence was not confined to the Hudson's Bay Company. In 1870 he was appointed by Prime Minister John A. Macdonald to sit on the first Council of the North West Territories and later that year he was elected to the first Provincial Assembly of Manitoba. This was followed, in 1871, by a successful bid to represent the riding of Selkirk as an Independent in the Dominion Parliament. Thus, in less than a decade, Smith had become firmly enmeshed in a national network of business, financial and political interests. It was during this period that Smith conferred with Cyril Graham who reported favourably on Smith's rapport with the commissioned officers. This, coupled with his obvious capabilities, was sufficient in Graham's eyes to recommend him for the position of the company's chief representative abroad.[17] As a result, Smith was appointed commissioner in June 1871 and chief commissioner a year later.

Smith's extensive background in the fur trade, combined with his business and financial expertise, suited him admirably for the task of spearheading Governor Northcote's campaign to revive the trade. Under Smith's local direction, the company proceeded with its programme of reorganization and increased capital investment. The success of his efforts was reflected in the dramatic rise in net trading profits in 1872 which were supplemented by the final payment of the Oregon settlement from the

---

[15]HBC, *Deed Poll by the Governor and Company of Hudson's Bay for Conducting their Trade in North America and for Defining the Rights and Prescribing the Duties of their Officers*, 1871, pp. 5-6.

[16]HBCA, A.33/5, fos. 190, 192.

[17]HBCA, A.11/100, fo. 32, Graham to Northcote, 31 January 1870.

American government in return for the surrender of the company's possessory rights in the Oregon Territory.[18]

Transportation was the key to efficient development of the company's resources. At that time there were two major routes to the North West. The Edmonton Trail, stretching overland from Fort Garry to Edmonton via Forts Ellice, Carlton and Pitt, functioned as the main supply artery for a radiating network of cart trails serving northern posts. However, under the proposed new scheme, the traditional water route linking the Red River, Lake Winnipeg and the Saskatchewan River was destined to become the primary supply route for the Northern and Western Departments. The company's first steamer, the *Chief Commissioner*, was launched on Lake Winnipeg in May of 1872, followed the next year by a riverboat on the Saskatchewan River. The *Chief Commissioner* subsequently proved unsuitable for navigation on the lake and it was replaced by the *Colvile*. After the riverboat ran aground in rapids near Cross Lake it was replaced by a sternwheeler, the *Northcote*, specially designed to cope with numerous rapids and fluctuating water levels that plagued the Saskatchewan River. Despite these initial setbacks it was hoped that steam transportation, coupled with ongoing development of the American railway system and the promise of a Canadian transcontinental line, would ensure higher profits for the company by halving the amount of time it took to ship goods to individual posts.[19]

Smith's tenure as chief commissioner was brief. His years in Labrador had not provided him with any practical experience in the management of inland transportation and his chronic habits of procrastination and haphazard record-keeping, dating back to his early days in the fur trade, gave rise to numerous complaints from senior commissioned officers.[20] Fortunately for Smith, the board was interested only in profits and dividends and his deficiencies as chief commissioner were masked by the satisfactory results of a slowly rising fur market. Despite the apparently favourable outlook, however, Smith was astute enough to realize the futility of depending solely on the fur trade for revenue. Growing optimism about the potential of the company's land tracts led the board to conclude that the task of administering both land and general trade was

---

[18]HBC, *Report*, 28 June 1872, p. 5. Net profits rose from £27,356 the previous year to £85,522.

[19]A.A. den Otter, "The Hudson's Bay Company's Prairie Transportation Problem 1870-1885" in John E. Foster (ed.), *The Developing West*, p. 28.

[20]NAC, *MacFarlane Papers*, fo. 263, Chief Factor Robert Campbell to MacFarlane, 14 September 1872; fo. 283, Chief Trader J. Lockhart to MacFarlane, 16 December 1872; fos. 301-328, Chief Trader Joseph Fortescue to MacFarlane, 25 May 1873; fos. 386-389, Fortescue to MacFarlane, 15 March 1874; fos. 392-397, Inspecting Chief Factor Robert Hamilton to MacFarlane, April 1874 cited in Robert Oleson, "The Commissioned Officers of the Hudson's Bay Company and the Deed Poll in the 1870's with Particular Emphasis on the Fur Trade Party, 1878-1879", pp. 65-67.

too burdensome for one man.[21]   In July 1873, Smith signed an article of agreement stating that effective 1 July 1874, he would be relieved of his duties in order to head up the company's land business under the newly created title of land commissioner reporting directly to London.[22]

Smith's successor was James A. Grahame, the former sub-commissioner who had been stationed in the Western Department and the man, some commissioned officers felt, who should have been given the position of chief commissioner from the start.[23]   He had joined the Hudson's Bay Company as an apprentice clerk at [Upper] Fort Garry in 1843 and was transferred the following year to Fort Vancouver. He was promoted to chief trader in 1854 and to chief factor eight years later when he moved to the Norway House District.[24]   In April 1872 he was appointed to the position of sub-commissioner.

In one of his first letters to the new chief commissioner, Deputy-Governor Eden Colvile warned Grahame of the precarious nature of his position, particularly with respect to his relations with Smith. Considerable tact would be required on Grahame's part to keep things working smoothly.

> You have sole and supreme authority over all clerks and servants in the fur trade and you must put a stop to any interference with this authority on the part of D.A. Smith or anyone else. Avoid giving offence and with a person of D. Smith's temperament this will require tact and management.[25]

All future correspondence with the Dominion government was to be directed through, or in concert with, Smith. Grahame was also cautioned against any political involvement. "We are now simply a trading corporation and wish to confine ourselves to our own business, cultivating the most friendly relations with those in authority but taking no side with one party or the other."[26]

---

[21]Evelyn Baril, "The Hudson's Bay Company and the Urbanization of the Prairies 1870-1888", p. 37.

[22]HBCA, A.33/5, fo. 196. Although Smith left the fur and general trade, he retained his ties with the commissioned officers and clerks as their investment broker.

[23]NAC, *MacFarlane Papers*, fo. 263, Chief Factor Robert Campbell to MacFarlane, 14 September 1872, cited in Oleson, "Commissioned Officers", p. 65.

[24]HBCA, A.33/3, fos. 155, 157. Also HBCA, Biographical File, James A. Grahame.

[25]HBCA, A.7/4, fos. 197-198, Colvile to Grahame, 15 June 1874.

[26]HBCA, A.7/4, fo. 199. Relations between the general public and the company had been strained by the company's apparent opposition to Winnipeg's bid for incorporation

(continued...)

The beginning of Grahame's tenure coincided with that of the new governor, George Joachim Goschen.[27] Committed to upholding a policy of heavy capital investment in the fur trade, from which the company could not withdraw without weakening its competitive edge over ever increasing numbers of free traders, Goschen considered the retention of vast land holdings to be a hazardous business venture. Private interest in its holdings was successfully used as an inducement to attract public interest and in 1875 the Dominion government, under Alexander Mackenzie, entered into negotiations with the company for the purchase of the bulk of its land holdings.[28] Negotiations and the depression dragged on with the company not wishing to appear an anxious seller and the government refusing to commit itself. By 1876, worsening economic conditions made it inadvisable to continue discussions and, with the return of a measure of prosperity and the Macdonald government in 1878, the purchase was never reconsidered.

Another of Goschen's plans to raise revenue stemmed from problems that the company had experienced with its initial introduction of steamers. The increasing number of vessels operating in the Western and Northern Departments were vital to the company's expansion program and it was imperative that they be protected. Consequently, Goschen announced that the company would fund a marine insurance scheme with money currently paid to outside interests which would prevent a further drain on profits by uninsured losses. The fur trade would be charged an annual fee which would be applied to the insurance fund and any sums deducted to cover losses would be debited to fur trade accounts. An initial amount of £40,000 was set aside despite the protests of shareholders who demanded to have it returned in the form of a dividend. The scheme was reluctantly approved but it continued to provide a steady source of revenue over succeeding decades.

Grahame's experience in both the Northern and Western Departments qualified him much better than Smith to oversee the reorganization of the company's transportation system. Despite initial setbacks, progress was being made in altering patterns which had evolved over the last century. In 1872, the Northern Pacific Railway reached Moorehead, Minnesota and ten years later it was announced that the bulk of Northern Department returns had been shipped by rail to New York, bypassing the historic Hudson Bay route. York Factory and Norway House, once central depots, quickly declined to simple trading posts serving the immediate area, and in 1878 the company's Canadian headquarters were

---

[26](...continued)
in 1873 in order to avoid taxation. The company owned approximately one third of the taxable land within the proposed city limits. Alan Artibise, *Winnipeg, A Social History of Urban Growth 1874-1914*, pp. 16-17.

[27]Goschen had served as First Lord of the Admiralty in the recently defeated British Liberal government. He was elected by the shareholders to replace Northcote upon the latter's return to British politics.

[28]HBC, *Proceedings*, 29 June 1875, p. 5.

removed from York Factory to Upper Fort Garry.[29] To the south, company steamers, having established a regular route along the Assiniboine in 1875, pushed the jumping-off point for cart brigades 230 miles west to Fort Ellice at the mouth of the Qu'Appelle River.[30] Their pre-eminence was short lived, however. The arrival of the railway in Calgary in 1883 finally ended long-distance carting on the Edmonton trail.

Although these were positive signs, the spectre of economic depression still loomed large. The spring fur sale of 1877 confirmed the downward trend. Fur prices tumbled 30 per cent below the previous year which had registered a twenty-year low. By fall there was an additional decline of 20 per cent in finer furs such as marten and mink in which the company specialized. The board authorized reductions in fur prices, but given the time lag in communicating information to individual posts, a considerable interval elapsed before prices could be adjusted. Faced with a loss of £2,911, the board declined to issue a dividend and the commissioned officers received no remuneration. At the same time, requisitions, which often had to be paid for two or three years in advance, were escalating to meet the demands of settlers, missionaries, government agencies and destitute Indians, as were Canadian duties on company imports and interest charges on its capital investment. In an attempt to adapt to altered circumstances, the board recommended revisions to the 1871 Deed Poll. The number of junior traders was increased from eight to twenty-one in hopes of attracting more qualified men who would eventually fill the upper ranks. Despite the board's efforts, economic conditions demanded greater emphasis on operational reorganization rather than administrative reform. The company was faced with two options: raise additional capital from its already disgruntled shareholders or close posts and withdraw from a portion of the business. The board chose the latter and curtailed credit sales, endorsed further withdrawal from unproductive posts and reduced investment in others which offered little assistance or protection to inland districts.

Cutbacks in transportation were not included. A new steamer, the *Lily*, had been added in 1877 to service the upper portions of the Saskatchewan River between Carlton and Edmonton leaving the *Northcote* to ferry supplies and returns between Carlton and Grand Rapids, the barrier to river navigation just above Lake Winnipeg. After years of debate, the board finally approved the construction of a tramway to bypass the rapids at a proposed cost of £4,000. Further improvements were planned with the introduction of small river steamers on the Athabaska River and Lake Winnipeg in the hope that, by the following year, the trade would reflect the benefits.

Unfortunately, the results of the 1878 spring sale were even more disastrous. Although the trade appeared to have finally rallied the next year, it was too late for the commissioned officers. After two years without their customary remuneration, they took matters into their own hands and mounted an aggressive campaign for a guaranteed

---

[29]See A.J. Ray, "York Factory: the Crisis of Transition, 1870-1880".

[30]A.B. McCullough, *Prices, Transportation Costs and Supply Patterns in Western Canada, 1873-85*, p. 375.

minimum income. Two years earlier they had succeeded in obtaining a temporary grant of £100 per share.[31] Looking for a more permanent arrangement, they organized under the name of the Fur Trade Party. Threatening mass resignation, the officers sent Chief Factor John H. McTavish and Donald A. Smith to present their demands to the board. Although Grahame, as chief commissioner, would have seemed a more logical choice than Smith, many officers believed that Grahame had refused to take the initiative on their behalf in the past and a rift between the two parties had developed.

The board acceded to all the officers' demands with the exception of a permanent guarantee of £150 per share. Instead, they received a minimum of £150 per share for Trading Years 77 to 81 (1879-1883). If fur trade profits exceeded £60,000 their portion would be increased to £200. In addition, the five unappropriated shares that had been applied to the retirement fund under the terms of the Deed Poll of 1871 would now be apportioned among the commissioned officers. Their satisfaction with the settlement was reflected in a conciliatory letter from the officers to Grahame in which they reaffirmed their confidence in him as their chief commissioner.[32] Their pleasure was short-lived, however. By 1879, the board was promoting general trade and land sales to the detriment of the fur trade and the importance of the commissioned officers to the organization steadily declined.

With the completion of the rail link between St. Paul, Minnesota and Winnipeg in 1878, cheap transportation links to major metropolitan centres became a reality. Although the era of steamboating on the Red River was over, the railway assured Winnipeg a role as distribution centre for western Canada. With the prospect of a Canadian transcontinental line, the company was finally in a position to expand its general trade into areas that would become important service centres for agricultural and urban settlements. It was obvious, however, that as immigration increased, changes would have to be made in the general trade. Most of the senior commissioned officers were natives of rural Scotland. Although they were well suited to the fur trade, they lacked a grounding in commercial principles and an appreciation for the needs of a new prairie society that were essential if the company wished to compete successfully.

As the decade came to a close, anti-company sentiment was again running high. Donald A. Smith was often criticized for not actively promoting land sales, preferring instead to wait until transportation improvements had increased values. The board finally agreed that, in the interests of public relations, the company's land policies needed reform.

Smith resigned as land commissioner in early 1879, his boundless ambition frustrated by a depressed land market. During his tenure he had often encroached on Grahame's jurisdiction, authorizing large capital investments in order to secure lucrative

---

[31]MTL, *Alexander Matheson Papers*, George Goschen to Commissioner James A. Grahame, private, 17 November 1877.

[32]GI, *Richard Hardisty Papers*, M5908, box 8, file 242, fo. 1611, commissioned officers to James A. Grahame, 12 July 1879.

government contracts and enhance land values. Such clashes demonstrated the need to resolve inherent conflicts among the company's senior officers in Canada.[33] Initial steps were taken by the board's appointment of Charles Brydges, the former General Superintendent of Railways under the Mackenzie government and political confidante of John A. Macdonald.[34] Although his official title was land commissioner, his mandate was much broader in scope as revealed in a confidential letter to Macdonald from board member Sir John Rose:

> I think you should know, in confidence, that our plan is to place Brydges in a position where he can - as he certainly very soon will -make himself master of the whole business, and ingratiate himself into the good opinion of the officers. This, however, must be done gradually, and Grahame and Smith must be used for a short time. Brydges - although nominally Land Commissioner - will really be instructed to feel his way as expeditiously as he can, so as to master the whole business of the Company - not only as regards the Lands, but as regards the Fur Trade as well ... Brydges is, in reality, the man who is to occupy the confidential relations, and exercise all authority from this day forward.[35]

This radical departure from the maintenance of control by London was characteristic of the increasing separation between ownership and management that occurred in business during the late nineteenth and early twentieth century.[36] Although HBC shareholders exercised their influence through an elected board of directors, formally known as the Governor and Committee, who were responsible for the development of general corporate strategy, management was passed to professional executives, such as Brydges, who were committed to maximizing the profits of their respective units. Brydges' private mandate ended the division of responsibilities in the

---

[33]Alan Wilson, "Introduction" in *The Letters of Charles John Brydges 1879-1882*, Hudson's Bay Company Land Commissioner, H. Bowsfield (ed.), p. xxv.

[34]Baril notes that when Smith resigned, the Board was prepared to abolish the position of land commissioner and instead have a clerk look after the lands. However, when Brydges offered his services, the specifications of the job were revised (PAM, *Macdonald Papers*, MG4B1-4, vol. 259, 10 February 1879, cited in Baril, "HBC and Prairie Urbanization", p. 77).

[35]NAC, *John A. Macdonald Papers*, vol. 191, Rose to Macdonald, confidential, 13 March 1879, cited in J.E. Rea, "Introduction" in *The Letters of Charles John Brydges 1883-1889*, H. Bowsfield (ed.), p. xxii.

[36]Ibid., pp. xxi-xxii. For a detailed examination of the rise of middle management and modern business enterprise after 1840 see Alfred D. Chandler's *The Visible Hand: The Managerial Revolution in American Business*.

company's Canadian operations, whereby each commissioner reported separately to London, and effectively streamlined the corporate structure.

Brydges' relations with Grahame, who remained unaware of the true extent of the land commissioner's mandate, were little better than Smith's had been. Brydges' suggestions that the retail trade should be expanded to take advantage of new opportunities and attract settlers were opposed by Grahame who preferred to be overcautious rather than incur heavy expense.[37] After a reprimand from the board, however, he promised to push such enterprises with vigour. As a result, the company proceeded to invest in new stores at Winnipeg, West Lynne and Portage la Prairie. Saw and grist mills were constructed in suitable locations in hopes of encouraging settlement, raising concerns for the future of the fur trade among many of the officers.

> What a fuss is made about mills, opening large and expensive stores &c at the cost of the fur trade, and for the benefit of the people at home [England]. They are pretty sharp those men at home, and in proposing mills etc. as they have done knew well that they would 'kill two birds with one stone' that is, keep the gross profits of the Trade under £60,000 so as to keep the guarantee at £150 per share, also to materially enhance the value of their land. I completely fail to see where any benefit is to come to the Trade through these undertakings. If the Trade could own the mills etc. I would then think it a reasonable speculation. As it is, we are simply making these improvements for the people at home at the immediate cost of the Trade and we allow them so many years to pay it in.[38]

Their fears were allayed somewhat by the election of a new governor, Eden Colvile, in 1880. Unlike his predecessors, who were noted more for their financial and political expertise, Colvile was familiar with the organization of the fur trade and had served for a brief period as governor of Rupert's Land. Also, unlike Goschen, he had the good fortune to take office at the beginning of a brief but spectacular land boom in the North West resulting from the choice of Winnipeg as the gateway to the west where the railway line crossed the Red River. Colvile immediately established friendly relations with the commissioned officers by touring the North West that summer. He discussed land and general trade issues with Brydges and Grahame and submitted a favourable report at the November 1880 annual shareholders meeting, or General Court.

One of the highlights of his report was the new Winnipeg store being constructed at York and Main to replace the aging Upper Fort, no longer considered suitable for a modern urban-oriented business. Four stories high, it boasted steam elevators and a wide

---

[37]HBCA, A.12/47, fos. 300-300d, Grahame to Armit, 16 September 1879.

[38]HBCA, E.39/3, fos. 16-16d. Chief Trader Ewen McDonald, Ile a la Crosse, to his brother A. McDonald, 8 March 1880, private.

variety of departments including dry goods, groceries, carpets, dressmaking, millinery, wines and liquors. The front was reserved for retail business and the back and upper floors for storage of furs and general merchandise. Chief Trader John Peebles was appointed manager and shareholders were assured that every effort had been taken to select qualified men from England to assist in running the business.

Despite admonitions from the board, relations between Brydges and Grahame were still strained. Brydges' aggressive campaign to expand the use of company steamers for government freight was repugnant to Grahame who remained firmly convinced that they should be reserved for the fur trade. He argued that carrying outside freight would interfere with crucial fur trade shipments and the uncertainty of water levels on the Saskatchewan River could leave the company open to costly damage claims for non-fulfilment of contracts should problems arise. The board supported Brydges' claim that if the company did not take the initiative in this area its competitors would, but it also ordered him to work more closely with Grahame.[39]

By 1880, company steamers were opened to public traffic and Brydges began to bid for government contracts. Competition was a major concern for it was feared that if other companies were allowed to operate they would corner the public business and gain access to prime fur trade areas. The company subsequently took controlling interest in the Winnipeg and Western Transportation Company and signed an agreement with its other major rival, the North West Navigation Company, giving the company controlling interest in all shipping on the Saskatchewan River system.

Negotiations were based on the assumption that the Canadian government would take steps to improve navigation on the Saskatchewan. Dredging was crucial to the system's reliability and its ability to compete with the Canadian Pacific Railway. The government, however, was more concerned with railway construction, and by the time the work was approved it was too little too late. By 1883, when the prairie section of the railway was completed, steamboats had been largely eclipsed although they remained an important feeder service north from the railway.

Anticipating the end of the agreement for a guaranteed remuneration in 1882, the commissioned officers petitioned to have it extended for an additional three years. The board approved the extension without the usual shareholders' debate, the latter having been appeased by a capital return of £2 per share accruing from land sales.[40] These gains were counterbalanced by a further erosion of the commissioned officers' power within the corporate structure. The board rescinded the clause in the resolution passed in 1879 entitling inspecting chief factors and chief factors to recommend officers to the board for promotion. By the terms of the new agreement, these recommendations were restricted to appointment of officers within the fur trade "exclusive of that branch of the

---

[39]den Otter, "Prairie Transportation", p. 34.

[40]HBC, *Report*, 17 June 1882, pp. 6, 10.

business in settled and partially settled Districts in which the general trade predominates."[41]

Brydges' fortunes waned with the collapse of the land boom in the spring of 1882. The board, becoming increasingly alarmed at the amount of capital expenditure involved in his plans for expansion, reverted to its original policy of a distinct separation between the land and trade departments. Grahame was now to be totally responsible for fur and general trade matters and careful research was to be undertaken before any recommendations for further expansion were made.

Complaints had reached the board implicating Brydges and Grahame in questionable dealings in company land. As a result, Deputy Governor Sir John Rose visited Canada with secretary William Armit and board member Sandford Fleming to investigate the allegations and to assess the company's position.[42] In his report, Rose concluded that the general trade could not remain viable under existing conditions. Upon visiting towns along the CPR, he noted the thriving business being conducted by independent traders from the United States and eastern Canada. Operating out of tents which could be easily moved to keep pace with construction, they carried a wide range of goods and had access by telegraph to suppliers in Winnipeg, St. Paul and Chicago who could fill orders within two days. In comparison, Rose described the situation at the company's post at Fort Qu'Appelle which was considered typical:

> The English goods had only arrived on the first week in July. The Canadian goods ordered the previous year had actually not come to hand at the date of our visit but were expected in carts from Fort Ellice. Many of the goods sent from England on requisitions prepared the previous year were unsuitable and a great demand existed for articles that had either not been ordered at all, or in insufficient quantities; some of them, such as potted meats, &c., having actually been procured from passing traders. When they run short at the store they have first to send a requisition by what is called express to the officer in charge of the district, at Fort Ellice (some 140 miles off). This, after it is examined and approved of there

---

[41]GI, *Richard Hardisty Papers*, M5908, box 8, file 248, fo. 1638, Armit to Grahame on behalf of the Governor and Committee, 24 October 1882.

[42]Sandford Fleming had been engineer-in-chief and super-intendent of the surveys for the CPR and was also a Director of that company. He became a HBC board member in 1882. He and Brydges had a long history of rivalry as railway advisors to the Dominion government. Brydges had criticized Fleming's engineering with the Intercolonial Railway and had clashed with Sir Charles Tupper, Fleming's mentor, and Fleming over their support for the Selkirk route through Manitoba as well as Tupper's support of a private contract for constructing the railway (Alan Wilson, "In a Business Way: C.J. Brydges and the Hudson's Bay Company, 1879-1889" in Berger and Cook, *The West and the Nation*, pp. 117, 122).

(which I am told takes some time), is forwarded by the usual cross-country road to Mr. Grahame [sic] in Winnipeg. The same process recurs there, and he sends the order perhaps to Montreal, St. Paul, Chicago or England. Many months elapse before the article - which the independent trader would in the meantime have turned over two or three times - arrives.[43]

Rose felt that there were few company officers, from the chief commissioner on down, who were competent to act as traders even if the board did grant them the power to act independently. Instead, the company needed a thorough and efficient businessman at the head of its trading operations. While he acknowledged that the company's prestige and reputation were widely recognized, Rose questioned whether it could turn this reputation to account. In his opinion, the company had two options: to confine its commercial operations to a wholesale general dealership in Winnipeg or to restrict itself to a small number of the best places where it could secure competent managers and avoid offending the commissioned officers. This would still require a strict and efficient head at Winnipeg and although Grahame "is a thoroughly trustworthy and upright man, deserving every consideration at our hands for his long and faithful services ... he has not the qualities fitting him for the new and varied duties that must be undertaken if we are to carry on an active commercial business."[44] He suggested instead, A. Conrad, one of the partners of Montana-based I.G. Baker & Sons, the company's chief competitor in the North West[45] or secretary Armit. He felt that the latter's selection might be viewed more favourably by the officers as it could be considered a promotion from within the service.

Rose also recommended that the company divest itself of its interest in bridges and the Winnipeg flour mill which was in need of costly modernization after six years of operation. As soon as the railway was established, he recommended that a similar policy be applied to the company's steamers.

Rose absolved Brydges of any involvement in the controversial purchase of the Upper Fort by Chief Commissioner Grahame, Sedley Blanchard, the company's solicitor, and another company officer who had planned to hold it for speculative purposes.[46]

---

[43]NLC, *Papers Relating to the Hudson's Bay Company*, confidential letter from Sir John Rose to the governor, 12 September 1882, p. 3.

[44]Ibid., p. 3.

[45]He was likely referring to Charles Conrad of I.G. Baker & Sons. See Chapter IV for a detailed discussion of the competition between the HBC and I.G. Baker.

[46]As a result of the land scandal, a resolution was passed by the board forbidding any officer, clerk, or surveyor from purchasing land belonging to the company without the express permission of the board (HBCA, A.1/152, fo. 40, 17 October 1882).

Grahame was not so fortunate. After reviewing statements from the participants, Rose concluded that Grahame's recollection of his role in the affair "was evidently entirely at fault".[47]   In March 1883, Governor Colvile requested that Grahame tender his resignation, stating that a younger and more active man was needed to run the business.[48] Grahame complied immediately but the board chose not to accept it, stating its unwillingness to terminate his long service so abruptly. Instead, he was asked to continue in his position for the present until his retirement could take place "at a time and a manner that would be agreeable to yourself and the Committee."[49] This placed Grahame in the unenviable position of having to maintain a facade knowing that he did not have the board's support or confidence and that he could be dismissed at any time. In the meantime, the board had effectively ensured his cooperation while it sought a successor. As a parting shot, Colvile informed Grahame that secretary Armit would be returning to Canada to carry out arrangements for the future conduct of the business. As a result of Armit's recommendations, Thomas R. [T.R.] Smith, the assistant secretary, was appointed to take temporary charge of the general trade.

Although Rose was a powerful ally, attacks on Brydges persisted from new quarters. At a shareholders' meeting, called in November 1883 to elect a new member to the board, Donald A. Smith voiced other shareholders' concerns regarding local management of both the land and commercial departments. He stated that land dealings at Fort Garry had not been made in the company's best interests and showed a lack of judgement which, in his opinion, called for an alternative form of supervision in Canada. Not enough money was being obtained for lots, especially those nearest the railway, and he described the conduct of the commercial business in Canada as "not such as would recommend itself to gentlemen concerned with commerce in England."[50] Although Smith was aware that the board had recently looked into these complaints, he called for a more thorough investigation which, in turn, was rejected by the board.

The election of directors took place and when the ballots were counted, it was discovered that Smith had staged a brilliant coup. Since there were no provisions in the Charter for voting by proxy, Smith had used his position as the major shareholder to nominate his own list of directors, which included himself.[51]   As his shares

---

[47]NLC, *Papers Relating to the HBC*, confidential letter from Sir John Rose to the governor, 12 September 1882, p. 4.

[48]GI, *Richard Hardisty Papers*, M5908, box 8, file 253, fo. 1670, Grahame to Hardisty, 10 June 1884.

[49]HBCA, A.7/5, fos. 98-99, Colvile to Grahame, 7 June 1883.

[50]HBC, *Proceedings*, 22 November 1883, pp. 9-10.

[51]HBCA, A.7/5, fos. 105-106d, Colvile to Sandford Fleming, 8 December 1883. Votes were apportioned by the amount of stock each shareholder held. For every £100 stock held, a shareholder was entitled to one vote and those with less could amalgamate
(continued...)

outnumbered those in support of the House List, the board decided to negotiate rather than risk a legal dispute. The result was an arrangement whereby Smith and one of his nominees were given seats on the board at a special General Court the following month and Smith and Sandford Fleming were requested to investigate the former's allegations concerning the company's Canadian operations.[52]

This was formalized on 1 May 1884 with the formation of a two-member Canadian subcommittee. Copies of all correspondence between North America and London, including the sale and disposition of lands, were to be submitted to the subcommittee and it was to approve all purchases of goods in North America. Satisfied that this would answer any complaints, the board ordered that any further enquiries into questionable land transactions be halted.

Having established a new administrative structure, the board set out in earnest to find a replacement for Chief Commissioner Grahame. Initial applications had proved disappointing. Casting further afield, board member Edward Harris contacted W.R. Haigh in Huddersfield who in turn approached an old and valued friend, Joseph Wrigley, who was seeking suitable employment. The Wrigley family had been involved in the wool trade in the Huddersfield area for several generations. After graduation from Rugby College, Joseph entered the family textile manufacturing business with his father and his younger brother, Norman. Following his father's death and a decline in demand for their specialized line of goods, the brothers reluctantly sold the business.[53]

Prior to his interview with the entire board, Wrigley was requested to provide additional personal information which might assist in making a decision. Although he admitted "it is not pleasant to speak of oneself", he stated that he was on the Commission of the Peace and had served as President of the Huddersfield Chamber of Commerce, "an office of considerable importance and consideration in that district." In addition he had taken part in semi-official commercial missions to Russia and France.[54]

At a meeting on 8 June the board agreed to appoint Wrigley to the position of trade commissioner at an annual salary of £1200. His appointment was for the standard five-year period, during which time he was not to engage in any business or trade outside the company or to undertake any public functions without the consent of the board. The latter could terminate his engagement with at least one year's notice and could dismiss him without notice for wilful neglect of duty or other misconduct.

---

[51](...continued)
(HBC, *Charters, Statutes, Orders in Council*, p. 28). On 9 September 1884 a supplemental charter was issued which allowed voting by proxy (ibid., pp. 31-32).

[52]NAC, *Sandford Fleming Papers*, MG29 B1, volume 96, folder 13, "Copy of a Resolution passed by the Governor and Committee on the 22nd January 1884", p. 1.

[53]HBCA, A.10/117, fo. 57d, W.R. Haigh to Edward Harris, 10 May 1884.

[54]Ibid. fos. 117-117d, Wrigley to Armit, 17 May 1884.

Grahame's resignation, tendered on 17 April 1883 was formally accepted on 11 June 1884 when he was informed of Wrigley's appointment. In a circular to the commissioned officers, he conceded that he resigned with some reluctance after nearly 42 years in the service.[55]

Wrigley's appointment reflected a trend towards a salaried system and away from the appointment of men to upper management positions from within the ranks of the fur trade. It was widely recognized that the company needed an infusion of new blood if it was to capitalize on the general trade. In particular, a man with broader commercial experience was needed to assume the duties of trade commissioner and there was no obvious successor to Grahame within the company's ranks.[56]

Wrigley's appointment, as anticipated by Smith, met with disapproval on the part of many of the old guard.[57] As early as July 1883, several of the commissioned officers had written to Grahame regarding rumours of his retirement stating

> It is needless for us to point out that the appointment of a Stranger to the Fur Trade and its Officers, would probably prove most injurious to our interests, besides creating much discontent and dissatisfaction among all in the Service - this belief is general, we might say almost universal, among the Commissioned Officers and we would therefore deprecate any change for the present.[58]

Others, such as Chief Factor Peter W. Bell, were more positive. Responding to the announcement of Wrigley's appointment, Bell offered his cordial cooperation, noting that the time had arrived when the company's commercial operations should be made remunerative. He revealed his true loyalties, however, in his statement that in the past the company had lavished thousands of pounds on stores, mills and steamers without adding to the dividend and if it were not for the fur trade, the fabric would not have been worth maintaining.[59]

---

[55]GI, *Richard Hardisty Papers*, box 8, file 253, fo. 1670, circular from James A. Grahame, 20 June 1884.

[56]Oleson, "Commissioned Officers", p. 249.

[57]NAC, *Sandford Fleming Papers*, MG29 B1, vol. 48, folder 331, D.A. Smith to Sandford Fleming, 19 August 1884.

[58]MTL, *Alexander Matheson Papers*, Chief Factor Richard Hardisty to Grahame, 7 July 1883. It was also signed by Chief Trader Lawrence Clarke, chief factors Roderick MacFarlane, Archibald McDonald, factors William McKay, Horace Belanger, J. McDougall, Ewen McDonald, chief traders J. Ogden Grahame, Alexander Matheson and junior chief traders G.S. Davison and James B. McKenzie.

[59]HBCA, A.10/117, fo. 544d. P.W. Bell to Armit, 21 August 1884. Bell would become one of Wrigley's chief detractors in later years.

What Wrigley faced, then, as he arrived in Winnipeg with his family[60] after brief orientation sessions in England and Montreal, was the daunting task of reorganizing the general trade on a more profitable basis while at the same time maintaining and streamlining the fur trade and transportation system on which the entire operation depended.

---

[60]Wrigley's first wife, Emilie Tillett, died of pneumonia soon after the family business was sold. Anne Ayre, the daughter of a doctor, was hired as housekeeper to help with Wrigley's five children, some of whom were "decidedly contrary." She and Wrigley were married shortly before leaving for Canada (correspondence with Dr. Joseph Wrigley, grandson).

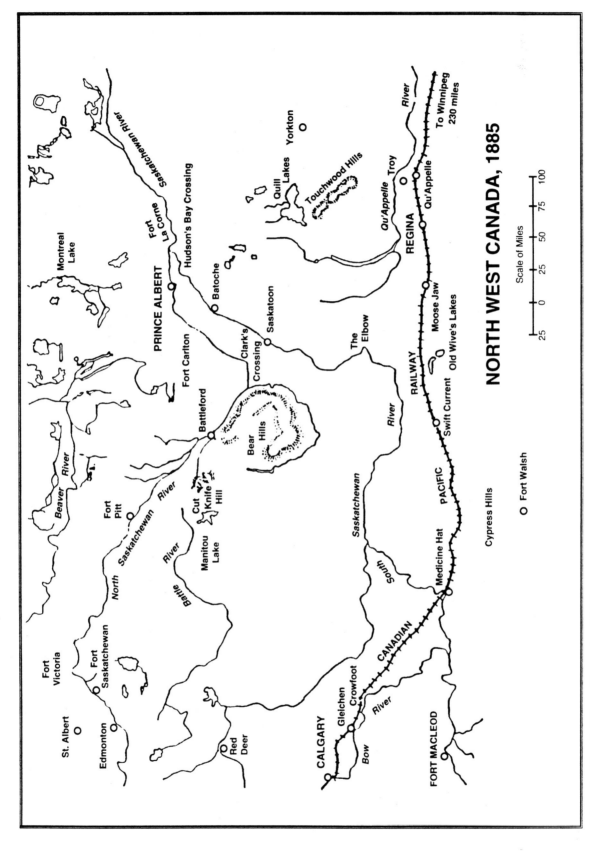

Map 1: North West Canada, 1885

Chapter 2

TROOPS, TRANSPORT AND TINNED BEEF: THE NORTH WEST REBELLION

Immediately upon his arrival in Winnipeg in August of 1884, Wrigley circulated a letter to the commissioned officers outlining the responsibilities of his new office. He asked for their support in carrying on the company's business, assuring them that they could write freely and confidentially on matters regarding the trade or their personal welfare.

He had little time to settle into the job. The North West was in a state of unrest and would soon erupt into violence, disrupting the company's plans for reform. With a major stake in the area, the Hudson's Bay Company and Wrigley could not avoid being deeply embroiled.

One of Wrigley's first correspondents was Chief Factor Lawrence Clarke, head of the Saskatchewan District. Clarke was in the midst of negotiations with the Dominion Government for housing for a detachment of Mounted Police that had been dispatched to Prince Albert in response to Louis Riel's recent return to the North West. Wrigley had been advised of the growing dissatisfaction among the "halfbreeds" in the North Saskatchewan district and echoed Clarke's concerns in his early correspondence to the London board.[61] Although Wrigley and Brydges visited Regina on 5 March 1885, they received no official report of trouble until two weeks later. Wrigley informed board Secretary William Armit that the "French halfbreeds", excited by Riel, were arming and had proclaimed the country closed effective 16 March.[62] Wrigley contacted Edgar Dewdney, Lieutenant-Governor of the North West Territories, who ordered Lt. Colonel Acheson G. Irvine, Commissioner of the N.W.M.P., north from Regina to Fort Carlton with a detachment of Mounted Police. Wrigley also sent instructions to Clarke to cooperate with the government but to leave responsibility to Ottawa and not to take more prominent action than was absolutely necessary.[63] He realized rightly that the main danger to the company lay in Riel's gaining the Indians' support but he reassured Armit

---

[61]HBCA, D.13/7, fo. 41, Wrigley to Armit, 3 November 1884 and HBCA, D.48/2, fos. 47-49, Clarke to Grahame, 20 May 1884.

[62]HBCA, D.13/7, fo. 150d, Wrigley to Armit, 19 March 1885.

[63]Clarke was considered an arrogant man and was actively disliked by many. He was suspicious of attempts by the Métis to organize and his rash behaviour was deemed partly responsible for the rebellion. He was alleged to have responded to Métis queries about the status of their petition and bill of rights with a threat that the government would send five hundred men to arrest Riel. Later, it was Clarke's taunts of cowardice that goaded Superintendent Leif N.F. Crozier into making the disastrous attack on Duck Lake without awaiting reinforcements (Bob Beal and Rod Macleod, *Prairie Fire, the 1885 North-West Rebellion*, pp. 139, 155. See also Stanley Gordon, "Lawrence Clarke" in *DCB*, vol. XI, p. 195).

that there was no cause for great uneasiness, "as the Government forces must be quite sufficient to deal with the matter if it should happen to assume a serious aspect."[64]

Military resources in Manitoba and the North West, under the command of Lt. Colonel Charles F. Houghton, were feeble at best.[65] A small permanent garrison in Winnipeg, the remainder of Colonel Garnet Wolseley's expedition of 1870, had been disbanded in 1877. The city had the only organized militia units in the west: the year-old 90th Rifles, a small battery of field artillery and a modest troop of cavalry.[66] In 1885, the Minister of Militia and Defence was Joseph Philippe René Adolphe Caron, a Quebec lawyer and close personal friend of the Prime Minister. At 42, he was the youngest member of Sir John A. Macdonald's cabinet, a man with no military experience but with many friends and political allies in the force. Militia and Defence was generally regarded as a patronage department and Caron had been selected for his political skills. After more than four years in office, the North West campaign was to be his first taste of serious responsibility.[67]

With no transport or support units Caron was forced to rely entirely on civilian assistance. To secure this aid, he approached Charles Brydges who was in Ottawa on business at the time. The Hudson's Bay Company was a natural choice given its established network of posts, personnel and transportation routes throughout the North West. However, this network also made it a prime target for rebel attack and it was therefore in the company's best interests to support any attempts by the government to quell the uprising. Brydges assured Caron that the company could provide everything necessary and, at the government's request, cabled Wrigley and informed Donald A. Smith of the arrangements.[68] The company was officially approached on 25 March. Wrigley was advanced $30,000 and a system was arranged whereby the government would be charged regular wholesale prices plus five per cent on all advances and payments for transport, wages and supplies.

Wrigley's worst fears were confirmed as reports reached him that a number of Indians had joined the uprising, cut telegraph wires and threatened Fort Carlton and Prince Albert.[69] Fear spread rapidly through the country as settlers armed themselves

---

[64]HBCA, D.13/7, fo. 151, Wrigley to Armit, 19 March 1885.

[65]Houghton, aged 47, was a former British army officer who had spent fourteen years on the militia staff in British Columbia and Manitoba. One official report described him as having "not much head and still less judgement" and he was an acknowledged drinker.

[66]Desmond Morton and Reginald H. Roy, *Telegrams of the North West Campaign 1885*, p. xxi.

[67]Ibid., pp. xxv-xxvi. See also Beal and Macleod, *Prairie Fire*, pp. 168-169.

[68]Bowsfield, *Letters of Brydges, 1883-1889*, p. 171.

[69]HBCA, D.13/7, fo. 153, Wrigley to Armit, 26 March 1885 regarding cable of 22 March, 1885.

against possible attack. In response, the government dispatched Major General Frederick Dobson Middleton to Winnipeg on 23 March.[70] Despite all this, Donald A. Smith remained confident. After conferring with Macdonald he assured Armit that he had

> no doubt Government will act promptly in restoring order, nor is it at all likely that there will be any difficulty in doing so the circumstances being so entirely different now with the great facilities for immediate dispatch of aid [the CPR] from those which existed at Fort Garry during the former disturbances.[71]

Wrigley was not as sanguine. As he informed Armit, "the crisis is grave and considering the stake the Company has in the country I feel confident that it will be the wish of the Board that everything possible should be done to assist the Government in restoring order."[72] Business in the entire south Saskatchewan region was seriously disrupted. The great unease caused by Riel's actions, Wrigley feared, would result in settlers withdrawing from farming operations as well as deter immigration needed as a market for the company's expanding commercial and land business.

Middleton arrived in Winnipeg on 27 March and immediately set out after Houghton for Fort Qu'Appelle with the remaining members of the 90th Battalion, leaving Wrigley 48 hours in which to get everything ready with no military liaison. Upon reaching his destination, Middleton appointed Samuel L. Bedson, warden of the Manitoba Penitentiary and former British soldier, as chief transport officer and Captain Herbert Swinford as chief commissariat officer. Lord Melgund, the future Earl of Minto, was appointed chief of staff and Chief Factor Archibald McDonald, in charge of Fort Qu'Appelle, was selected to hire teams. A major problem was that both Bedson and Swinford were under Middleton's orders and did not answer to Caron.[73] Matters were further complicated with the appointment of Major William R. Bell, a former Canadian militia officer, to the position of Quartermaster at Qu'Appelle with orders to obtain wagons, horses and forage. As one of the founders and manager of the Qu'Appelle Valley Farming Company, a large commercial farm near Indian Head, he became one

---

[70]Middleton, at age 60, had seen extensive military action around the world but had never been in western Canada. He joined the British Army in 1842, fought in the Maori war in New Zealand, distinguished himself in the Indian Mutiny of 1857-58 and served as commandant of the military college at Sandhurst from 1874 to 1884. As an alternative to immediate retirement on half pay, he accepted the appointment of Major General of the Canadian Militia, a post which was not considered particularly demanding (Beal and Macleod, *Prairie Fire*, p. 170, pp. 220-221).

[71]HBCA, A.12/53, fo. 94, Smith to Armit, 24 March 1885.

[72]HBCA, D.13/7, fo. 163d, Wrigley to Armit, 30 March 1885.

[73]J.E. Rea, "The Hudson's Bay Company and the North-West Rebellion", p. 47.

of the major suppliers of teams for the militia as well as one of its major contractors, which constituted an obvious conflict of interest.

By 28 March transport and supplies for 30 days had been dispatched. Noting that the company's stock of goods had been greatly diminished and that demands for provisions were already coming in from Fort Carlton, Wrigley requested an estimate from Caron of the number of reinforcements being sent from the east. He expressed concern that the area north of Qu'Appelle could not be depended on as a source of supplies forcing the company to look to the United States for goods which he hoped would be allowed to cross the border duty-free.

Three days after the company accepted the role as primary supplier to the government's troops, organization was still chaotic. Wrigley assured Caron that despite the fact that there was no supply officer in Winnipeg, incoming troops would be provisioned once particulars regarding time and point of delivery were received. The company had already incurred over $76,000 worth of debts and his request to draw an additional $30,000 was granted.

Although Wrigley stated that the company was buying from outside sources as cheaply as possible, his efforts were hampered by merchants anxious to capitalize on the situation. Alexander Galt, head of North-West Coal and Navigation Company, telegraphed Caron to place his flotilla of steamboats and barges located at Medicine Hat at the minister's disposal. In the same breath he added,

> As you will want large supplies of canned goods, groceries, etc. from Winnipeg, I wish you would bear in mind that my son Jack is in business there and has the largest assortment of wholesale articles of this kind. His firm is GT and J Galt and you may depend on all they undertake to do . . . . Pray do this for me.[74]

Amos Rowe, editor of the Winnipeg *Times*, wired the Honourable Mackenzie Bowell, petitioning him to instruct Wrigley to give the contract for biscuits and bread to Thomas Chambers as "he is a good conservative and brother-in-law to Colonel Kennedy. The man that has it now are [sic] Grits and bad ones at that."[75] Kenneth Mackenzie, president of the Winnipeg Board of Trade and Conservative MLA, wrote to John A. Macdonald that owing to the utter prostration of business in the area due to the present troubles, the wholesale merchants wished the government to purchase commissariat

---

[74]NAC, *CP*, Galt to Caron, 30 March 1885, p. 79. Alexander T. Galt, one of the Fathers of Confederation, served as Canada's High Commissioner in London from 1880 to 1883. He had invested substantially in the North West, particularly in the coal industry. The Hudson's Bay Company also had a fleet of steamers but the majority of them were wintering at Prince Albert behind rebel lines.

[75]Ibid., Amos Rowe to Caron, 13 April 1885, p. 263.

supplies locally wherever possible as all their stocks were large.[76] His complaints were echoed by Joseph Royal, Conservative member of Parliament for Provencher, who warned Caron of the Winnipeg business community's dissatisfaction with the HBC's monopoly on supply contracts. Caron, in turn, advised Wrigley to obtain supplies from Winnipeg merchants wherever possible to allay any bad feelings.

Confusion still reigned in early April when Wrigley received word that an additional 2200 men were expected to arrive. Was the company to provision them? Also, a local paper had reported that the government had contracted with Armour Packing Company of Chicago to supply tinned meat, a rumour that Caron denied, reassuring Wrigley that no contracts had been made with any other company.[77] On 2 April Lt. Colonel W.H. Jackson arrived in Winnipeg as principal supply officer. His instructions were to form a commissariat corps to take responsibility for transport, payments and supplies for the force. Although his appointment helped to streamline the chain of command some uncertainty remained. In response to Caron's orders to direct all requisitions through Jackson, Wrigley replied,

> There must be some mistake - can send rations of provisions when ordered but have been stopped. There must be somebody here to give instructions. Jackson says he has no authority and if I had not acted on my own responsibility, trouble would have been caused. No difficulty if you will arrange for us to receive instruction. Urgently call your attention to this.[78]

As a result, Jackson received full authority to issue requisitions that same day.

Events had their humorous side as well. After ordering 100,000 pounds of canned beef from the Armour Packing Company, Wrigley received a warning from Caron to beware of tinned meat from the Chicago-based company. He had received information that it had been poisoned by Fenians who had targeted another purchaser, the British government. Caron suggested, instead, that live cattle be purchased from Montana-based I.G. Baker & Sons and other western suppliers. A flurry of telegrams ensued, each party reluctant to take responsibility. Finally, after a satisfactory provincial analyst's report was issued and the troops' needs had become almost desperate, the meat was forwarded.

The provision of fresh beef continued to be a pressing issue. The *Free Press* reported complaints about the poor quality of food and clothing at the front. The editorials did not find fault with the suppliers as the goods in question were exactly what had been ordered. Rather, they attacked the government for not ordering anything more

---

[76]Ibid., K. Mackenzie to Macdonald, 30 March 1885, p. 110.

[77]*Winnipeg Daily Times*, 1 April 1885.

[78]NAC, *CP*, Wrigley to Caron, 5 April 1885, p. 157.

palatable than hardtack and bacon.[79] Wrigley and Jackson discussed the logistics of driving cattle north to the front and concluded that although they could be purchased for one third the price of canned meat, extra drivers and horses would be required at a time when both were in extremely short supply. Shrinkage of cattle on the march and uncertainty of fodder presented extra problems that made it more desirable to contract out for fresh beef. Caron, influenced by reports of volunteers' complaints in the Winnipeg *Times*, recommended that contracts be made with Gallagher and Sons as, in Amos Rowe's words, they were "good men".[80]

Despite the arrival of Jackson, the situation remained chaotic. By 7 April, Wrigley had still not been advised exactly how many men to provide for, the length of time they were to be supplied and what provisions to buy. There would be no difficulty in meeting demands he informed Caron, but until specifics were available, he was operating in the dark. In response, Caron informed him that 2,450 men were on the move and Wrigley was to provide for them and an equal number of horses for one month. Wrigley and Jackson countered with a plan to stockpile rations for five thousand men for two months. Only on Caron's insistence did Wrigley reluctantly agree to thirty days, noting however that merchants were already buying up goods on speculation and prices were rising rapidly. Finally, after dogged persistence on Wrigley's part, Caron agreed to establish a Winnipeg depot to facilitate the filling of large requisitions that were coming in without notice and requiring immediate execution. However, he firmly vetoed a recommendation to establish an independent commissariat to supply Major General Thomas Strange in Calgary, which had only weekly rail contact with Winnipeg. Strange was instructed to requisition supplies from Winnipeg as was Lt. Colonel William Otter, who was based in Swift Current.

Wrigley placated Winnipeg merchants by buying nothing from outside Winnipeg with the exception of the infamous tinned meat. By mid-April he reported that anti-company sentiment was abating, assisted by a donation of £500 to the Volunteer Relief Fund on behalf of the London board and an additional $100 in Wrigley's name.[81] He added that the major problem was not, as Caron had suggested, in the distribution of contracts but in the avoidance of inferior articles which would cause a great outcry if sent to the troops and would reflect poorly on the Hudson's Bay Company.

As expenses continued to mount, Wrigley tried to mollify Caron whose balance sheet was being closely scrutinized by both John A. Macdonald and the Opposition. He assured Caron that the company was purchasing at the lowest price possible, paying immediate cash and charging the government only a small commission. In no case were company prices more than Winnipeg market price. The total cost, he concluded, was

---

[79]*Manitoba Free Press*, editorials, 6 April and 7 April 1885.

[80]They were Winnipeg butchers who were considered reliable party supporters.

[81]The *Free Press* reported that the relief fund was started with individual $5,000 donations from Donald A. Smith and George Stephen (*Manitoba Free Press*, 4 April 1885).

far less than would be the case if the government created its own organization which, indeed, would take a long time to mobilize.

In official reports to the London board, Wrigley expressed concern about the difficulties faced by the militia. He feared that the rebels would employ guerilla warfare tactics rather than meet in an open fight. He noted a feeling of sympathy towards their cause in some quarters that could swell, with serious political repercussions, especially if Middleton met with a decided reverse.[82] Although Wrigley tried to remain apolitical in his dealings, he could not refrain from expressing regret that sufficient enquiry had not been made into the justice of the Métis' claims: "in fact, discontent in the North-West has increased to such an extent that had not this outbreak occurred it is not impossible that there might have been trouble even in Manitoba."[83]

Once the supply problem was more or less settled, Wrigley turned his attention to transportation. Gaps in the railway presented only one of many logistical problems which had been circumvented by shipping ammunition, horses and baggage over American routes through Detroit and Chicago. Spring arrived late that year in central and western Canada. Although this allowed troops to cross gaps along the north shore of Lake Superior on ice roads it played havoc with mobilization. Hearing that the Saskatchewan River was open on 28 March, Caron ordered the *Northcote* to be readied at Medicine Hat to ferry troops northward, but this information was premature by at least a week. Middleton grumbled that the rebels had chosen the worst possible time when roads and rivers were nearly impassable and all teams would be urgently required for seeding. The major transport problem would be expense, "which I fear would be enormous though I do all I can to keep it down. Everybody seems to think the government fair prey, and the long distance away from the Railway necessitates so much team transport, and that is so expensive."[84] A prime factor was the cost of forage, as it was too early in the year for grazing and hay had to be hauled overland.[85] Jackson cabled Caron on 19 April that although there were large quantities of hay on hand at Troy and Fort Qu'Appelle, there was a shortage of teams for hauling beyond the

---

[82]HBCA, D.13/7, fo. 167d, Wrigley to Armit, 6 April 1885.

[83]Ibid., fo. 172, Wrigley to Armit, 13 April 1885.

[84]NAC, *CP*, Middleton to Caron, 8 April 1885. Four major wagon trails led off from the CPR to Fort Pitt and Prince Albert varying in length from 279 to 398 miles (Department of Militia and Defence, *Report of Lt.-Col. W.H. Jackson*, p. 37). Supply routes were divided into 20 mile stages with an assistant transport officer in charge of each (C.A. Boulton, *Reminiscences of the North-West Rebellions*, p. 396). Over 100 teams would leave base camp and ten teams would be dropped off at each post along the way.

[85]Bedson estimated that each team could consume 80 pounds of oats and 30 pounds of hay per day (NAC, *Extracts from Lord Melgund's Journal*, NW Campaign, Transport Supply Report, n.p., n.d.).

Touchwood Hills. By 24 April the situation had worsened. Baled hay was selling for $30 a ton at Qu'Appelle and loose hay for $25. Wrigley succeeded in obtaining permission to import hay from the United States but only if it could be purchased at a lower price. Meanwhile Middleton had been halted at Carlton Crossing for lack of forage, the troops having moved so quickly that transport teams could not keep up the pace.

The cost of team transport was also cause for concern. By 20 April, Wrigley estimated that the company had spent over $100,000 on provisions and stores, a figure which was increasing daily. He had laid out advances of up to $70,000 for teams and hay, had drawn on the government for $110,000 and was asking for another $100,000. Since remittances were not coming in from company posts during the rebellion, he also requested to draw on London for £10,000.

Caron queried reports that the company was paying between seven and eight dollars a day for teams which had originally been hired for three dollars a day, with middlemen pocketing the difference. Wrigley protested that they could not be obtained more cheaply and the company was obliged to allow some margin of profit to contractors as the teams were gathered from across the country. By 24 April Wrigley reported that although there were 1000 teams working, he had received a cable from Quartermaster Bell at Qu'Appelle that they were failing to keep up with demand and were beginning to play out. Bell calculated that of 450 teams on the Qu'Appelle route, 160 were with the general's advance. To feed both them and the men would take another 800 teams and they had but 300. Although an additional 300 could be raised over the next few days he feared that no more would be available unless American teams were hired.[86] Consequently, Caron authorized a contract for an additional 24 ox teams with I.G. Baker & Sons.

The last regiment left Winnipeg on 29 April. Colonel Jackson was ill with pleurisy and no one had authority to take his place. The government owed $100,000 for supplies forwarded on requisition and an additional $150,000 for teamsters.

To economize, Wrigley suggested that the Winnipeg firm of Boyd & Crowe be given a contract to construct flatboats to transport freight from Saskatchewan Landing, 25 miles north of Swift Current, to Clarke's Crossing. Middleton supported the proposal as it would cost one quarter the expense of teams. He had advised Caron that land transportation between the two points was a serious problem particularly as the destination was so far from the railway. The *Northcote*, laden with troops and supplies, was fighting a constant battle with low water levels on the South Saskatchewan and was stranded frequently on sandbars, causing Middleton to comment later that it came mostly by land. Consequently, all teams that could be spared from Colonel Otter's column were rerouted over the Moose Jaw Trail to Clarke's Crossing, loading up en route with supplies from the *Northcote* at the elbow of the South Saskatchewan River. By 2 May, the immediate crisis was over and the transport officer cabled Wrigley that no further teams were needed.

---

[86]NAC, *CP*, Wrigley to Caron, 24 April 1885, p. 315.

Arrangements had yet to be completed for the use of the *Northcote*. General Middleton had been unable to finalize details with the company before his departure. Wrigley chose to leave the matter in Caron's hands asking, "would you prefer to charter her or leave for present question of payment on understanding she is on Government service?"[87] After several days of negotiations Wrigley agreed to a rate of $250 per day including expenses. Elliott Galt, manager of the North-West Coal and Navigation Company in Lethbridge, was less reticent. With all his steamers and barges now actively engaged he asked for $1000 per day or $600 plus expenses in addition to a guarantee of indemnity from rebel damage.[88]

Caron continued to press for economy in land as well as water transport. After being informed by Wrigley that the hire price for teams already in service ranged from $6.50 to $10 per day, Caron queried if they could be secured at lower rates if a tender system was adopted. He also suggested substituting cheaper priced teams. Wrigley agreed but cautioned that Lake Winnipeg was expected to break in three weeks which would allow goods to be shipped by water to Prince Albert, Battleford and Edmonton. The more expensive teams could then be dismissed without having to be replaced by inexperienced men who might fail to make prompt delivery. Also, since most of these new men would be Americans, the move to dismiss Canadians would be unpopular.

Colonel Jackson supported Wrigley's arguments, pointing out that the cost of bringing in new teams and discharging old ones would be more than the money saved in wages. The main problem in cancelling contracts was that they contained a clause that teams must be immediately transported back to their point of hire. This provision was expensive but its omission would prevent many experienced teamsters from tendering on new contracts. All the expensive teams were with General Middleton and it would take at least three weeks to replace them. Finally, Caron left the decision in Wrigley's hands.

Two days later, however, Caron was again advising Wrigley to cut expenses if it could be done without interfering with the level of service. Wrigley reiterated that the company did not have the authority to dismiss teams. Its duty was to provide and pay teams requisitioned by the military and these teams were entirely at the military's disposal. Unsatisfied, Caron authorized Chief of Staff Lord Melgund to examine the transport and supply situation on his return to Ottawa from Qu'Appelle and dispatched Lt. Colonel Whitehead, a Montreal businessman on the Retired List, to Winnipeg as chief transport officer to relieve Jackson who was still ailing.

Whitehead assured Caron that he would act with discretion in reorganizing the transport system which he complained was "all wrong". Noting the obvious conflict of interest Whitehead wrote, "Is Major Bell of the Bell Farm a contractor serving two masters viz himself and the Government?"[89] and refused to issue requisitions on his orders. Wrigley argued that he had called attention to the high costs many times. He

---

[87]Ibid., Wrigley to Caron, 2 May 1885, p. 352.

[88]Ibid., Galt to Caron, 6 May 1885, p. 385.

[89]Ibid., Whitehead to Caron, 15 May 1885, p. 423.

suggested several options: contract for transportation by the ton instead of by the day, reduce penalty costs for terminating contracts, or wait two weeks and dismiss several hundred teams when the river opened. If Caron wished, the company would stand aside and hand over supplies now in the depot but, he warned,

> I must remind the Government that, at their request, the Company at a moment's notice came to their assistance with their whole organization and have worked incessantly not so much for money as [to be] of assistance in subduing the Rebellion. A change now would be looked upon as placing the company in a position with regard to the public I cannot think the Government contemplate.[90]

Mounting pressure on Caron was reflected in his curt reply: "Still think for protection of Department all should be done by tender and expect you to help me in carrying this out. Company of course can tender like anybody else."[91] Caron ordered existing transport contracts cancelled and new teams engaged directly in order to save the contractors' markup.

Telegrams flew between Winnipeg and Ottawa, Caron ordering Wrigley to cancel all contracts while Wrigley protested that the company did not have the authority. This elicited Caron's confused reply, "I am under impression transportation under your control - who manages this?"[92] Caron argued that Whitehead had been appointed Transport and Supply Officer and by working through him, considerable savings could be effected without disturbing efficiency.

Wrigley's counter-proposal demonstrated a more astute grasp of the situation. Transport, he argued, should be the responsibility of an officer under Middleton's immediate control for only he knew the exact requirements. He pointed out that many teams had been hired during a time of emergency and that middlemen were needed as it was seeding time and overland travel was difficult. In any case, winter rates, at which the early teams had been hired, were always double the summer rates. He warned Caron to beware of the tender system as, in his experience, some made offers but didn't produce. "Fully understand difficulties of Department," he continued, "but from late experience and see & hear, however Department may strive, great difficulty and trouble will most likely prevail to an extent which would make Company fear to tender."[93] He defended the company, reminding Caron that it had supplied teams as they were required and then passed control over to the military transport officer. The system had worked well but now there were too many government officials whose authority clashed.

---

[90]Ibid., Wrigley to Caron, 16 May 1885, p. 438.

[91]Ibid., Caron to Wrigley, 18 May 1885, p. 438.

[92]Ibid., Caron to Wrigley, 19 May 1885, p. 450.

[93]Ibid., Wrigley to Caron, 20 May 1885, p. 455.

"By Transport Officer do you mean Bedson? Who are Government officials whose authority clash[es]?" replied a still-confused Caron. Whitehead, as far as he was concerned, was solely authorized by the government. Wrigley then requested clarification as to whose orders the company should follow, Bedson's or Whitehead's as they often conflicted: "we will do anything if we only know what is wished as management of teams in field is not in our province."[94]

Complaining that Wrigley had not yet cancelled team contracts Whitehead fumed to Caron:

> This ruse on the part of Wrigley [citing legal obligations] is to cause delay which is to his Company's advantage. I am willing to give them the preference for future contracts but they are not willing to resign their present hold and throwing obstacles in the way. In meantime running on tonnage system in spite of him at great saving. Suggest you telegraph then that I have full power to relieve them and insist on immediate cancelling.[95]

Caron was of no help on this point. He admitted to Middleton that he never knew that Major Bell was employed by the government or that Bedson was in charge of transportation. Accountability was his only concern. As he fretted to Middleton, "I need not tell you that I am anxious that all charges which will be submitted to Parliament be such that they can bear the light of day."[96]

Complaints were also being received from the teamsters themselves. One of the major suppliers, Armit and Kelly, condemned the manner in which their teams were being returned. Teams of which they had no knowledge were being shipped to them while theirs were sent elsewhere making it impossible to get them back by rail without needless delay. In other cases, drivers returned from Swift Current claiming that their teams had been sold while, in fact, they were still engaged by the military on work for which contractors demanded payment.[97] Teams that had been given notice by the

---

[94]Ibid., Wrigley to Caron, 10 May 1885, p. 456.

[95]Ibid., Whitehead to Caron, 21 May 1885, p. 461. Wrigley was supported by Sedley Blanchard, the company's solicitor. He stated that the company was responsible for payment as, by the terms of their contract, contractors had no recourse to the government. The contract could only be cancelled by return of teams to the point of delivery, the contractor being entitled to payment up to the time of final delivery. Cancellation meant that all of a contractor's teams must be returned, they were not bound to take them in instalments (HBCA, D.15/4, fos. 274-275d, Blanchard to Whitehead, 21 May 1885).

[96]NAC, *CP*, Caron to Middleton, 22 May 1885, p. 462.

[97]HBCA, E.9/3, fos. 85-86d, Armit & Kelly to HBC, 9 June 1885.

company had subsequently been rehired by the government. Since many of the original contracts provided for return to Winnipeg some contractors claimed that the first contract had not legally been terminated and demanded compensation.

By 22 May Whitehead was able to report that contracts had been cancelled by the company, teamsters had been legally notified and tenders were being forwarded to Caron for approval. With transportation problems more or less resolved, he could now turn his attention to reorganizing the supply system and call for tenders. He warned Caron, "You are surrounded by thieves. Supplies have been sent forward sufficient for 20 thousand troops - the waste is ruinous."[98] The entire supply department was "disgusting" and it appeared to him that all parties were using the rebellion as an excuse to make all they could. He reported, however, that in two weeks all supplies would be delivered to the front and the teams at Qu'Appelle, Moose Jaw and Swift Current could be discharged.

After three weeks in office, Whitehead was still complaining that the Hudson's Bay Company was executing orders from the front without consulting him. He argued that he had to be in sole control in order to run an efficient system and advised that the company be relieved of its authority as he was well able to handle any small requisitions that might come in.[99] Wrigley was advised that Whitehead now had sole control of ordering supplies, but by then he appeared to have washed his hands of the whole business. When Caron communicated his intention to keep him informed regarding the tenders he replied non-committally, "Thanks for the telegram. Shall be glad to hear results of tenders, am almost as anxious as you for success, and if you will privately tell me what I can do I will cordially co-operate with you but now I hear little about either transport or supplies."[100]

By mid-May, with Batoche taken and Riel captured, Wrigley was looking to the future. Although it was not yet possible to estimate the company's losses on buildings and property, he suggested that the London board seek legal advice prior to submitting a claim to the government.[101] Such precautions were not premature, for on 18 May a group of Cree pillaged the company's post and freighting depot at Green Lake where supplies for the Athabaska and Mackenzie Districts were over-wintered. At that time the warehouse held 190,000 pounds of supplies including guns and a large quantity of ammunition but losses were reduced due to the foresight of James Sinclair, the post clerk, who cached most of the furs and ammunition along the banks of the river. The following day the store at Lac la Biche was raided.

Wrigley had more immediate problems, however. With questions from the Opposition mounting, Caron insisted that all vouchers be sent to him before he accepted any more drafts. Wrigley protested that vouchers could take months to process since

---

[98]NAC, *CP*, Whitehead to Caron, 24 May 1885, p. 471.

[99]Ibid., Whitehead to Caron, 13 June 1885, p. 508.

[100]Ibid., Wrigley to Caron, 16 June 1885, p. 514.

[101]HBCA, D.13/7, fo. 186, Wrigley to Armit, 11 May 1885.

signatures were often difficult to obtain but teamsters had to be paid immediately. For example, he knew of $80,000 worth of vouchers awaiting signature at Calgary as no one had been authorized to sign for General Strange who had left for Edmonton on 20 April en route to Fort Pitt.[102]

With no money forthcoming, Donald A. Smith placed further pressure on Caron but to no immediate avail. On Smith's assurance that if vouchers equalling one quarter of the desired draft could be produced, approval would follow, Wrigley prepared to draw the requisite funds. But Caron met his request with a curt "Don't draw until I tell you . . . . Mr. Smith is under misapprehension."[103] Only after Wrigley pointed out that if he told the teamsters that they would not be paid, it would reflect poorly on the government, did Caron reluctantly issue a draft for $250,000, a sum raised later that day to $350,000 after a personal visit from Smith. A further draft of $250,000 was promised in 30 days.[104] For his part, Wrigley assured Caron that vouchers would be forwarded without delay and company employees, such as Lawrence Clarke, would be warned to pay nothing without obtaining vouchers with authorized signatures.

By late August Lt. Colonel Jackson (chairman), Lt. Colonel Whitehead, and Lt. Colonel W.H. Forrest, paymaster and superintendent of stores at Quebec, had been appointed to a war claims commission to investigate all outstanding accounts. The government's intentions were made clear in a private letter to Jackson.

> Every claim must be gone into and I trust to you to cut down without mercy. The country will stand by you and we need not be anxious about any little dissatisfaction arising among those who may be disappointed as to the amount they shall receive . . . . You need have no hesitation in using the knife.[105]

Once the commission was appointed Caron refused to accept further drafts from the Hudson's Bay Company or anyone else. Wrigley, in turn, protested that the drafts were not to satisfy outstanding claims but to cover payments already made in the North West on the government's authorization. Continued refusal on Caron's part prompted Wrigley to make personal appeals to the government, to the manager of the Ottawa

---

[102]NAC, *CP*, Wrigley to Caron, 16 June 1885, p. 512.

[103]Ibid., Caron to Wrigley, 17 June 1885, p. 516.

[104]Ibid., Caron to Wrigley, 18 June 1885, p. 519. A statement of payment and supplies to 19 June totalled $1,067,604 against which the company had drawn $960,000 (HBCA, D.15/4, fo. 359, Wrigley to Caron, 25 June 1885). Wrigley estimated that further requirements were likely to total another half million with a total profit to the company of between £15,000 and £20,000.

[105]NAC, *CP*, Caron to Jackson, 21 August 1885, p. 620.

branch of the Bank of Montreal, and to Donald A. Smith.[106] Even Whitehead advised Caron to modify his stance as "there had begun feeling here in consequence which is not doing our party any good."[107] Finally, on 29 September, Caron authorized a draft of $100,000 to the company.

Reassured, Wrigley turned his attention to company business which had been neglected during the rebellion. However, upon his return from a month in the Western Department, he discovered that nothing had been paid during his absence. Renewing his requests to Ottawa, Wrigley threatened to report to the London board unless his just demands were met. By 17 November he had received an additional $100,000 with the balance of between seventy and eighty thousand dollars to be paid once the war claims commission's investigations had been concluded.[108] Cables were exchanged at weekly intervals with Wrigley insisting that the money owed was a debt, not a claim for losses, while Jackson and Whitehead advised Caron to advance no more than $25,000. The tiresome campaign for compensation finally concluded in February 1886 when the company received a settlement of $65,471.05.[109]

Negotiations for the settlement of the company's rebellion losses claim were equally protracted. Solicitor John Bain presented his first report to Wrigley in early November 1885 upon his return from an inspection tour of Saskatchewan. He recommended that the company claim $168,053.05 in damages to which he added $40,305.88 to cover the cost of transportation, supplies furnished to Indians and food for refugees for a total of $208,358.93.[110]

To estimate claims, Bain used the cost of goods and merchandise at the place where they were pillaged. He concluded that the fairest settlement for furs was to charge the government London prices minus what it would cost to ship the furs to London. Since it would take several months to determine London fur prices, however, he based the claim on average prices over the last three years, leaving the final decision in the board's hands.

In forwarding Bain's recommendations to the board, Wrigley cautioned that any unnecessary delay would only hurt the company's case. In the interests of expedience he supported Bain's suggestion that furs be valued at an average price. He also agreed that claims for goods be calculated at cost landed, which was the only system that the

---

[106]Desmond and Roy, *Telegrams*, F. Gundry, Manager, to Caron, 8 September 1885, p. 404. NAC, *CP*, Wrigley to Donald A. Smith, 14 September 1885, p. 629.

[107]Ibid., Whitehead to Caron, 22 September 1885, p. 631.

[108]HBCA, D.13/7, fo. 290. Wrigley to Armit, 17 November 1885.

[109]NAC, *Military Papers*, vol. 159, Jackson to Minister, 16 February 1886 cited in Rea, "The HBC and the North-West Rebellion", p. 56.

[110]HBCA, E.9/28, fos. 30-33.

commissioned officers could understand, despite the fact that it did not take interest or expenses into account.[111]

With regard to serious accusations which had been made against members of the Police force, Wrigley noted that the company was on excellent terms with them and held most of their contracts. Therefore, although both police and troops had returned laden with company furs taken from Métis and Indians, Wrigley cautioned the board to refrain from pursuing the matter as he was sure that it would wish to avoid issues that might lead to ill feeling.

In reply, the board directed Wrigley to add 25.5 per cent to the valuation of goods at cost landed to bring the amount up to actual sale price. This figure was based on interest over eighteen months at 6 per cent, 12 per cent for transportation costs and 4.5 per cent for shrinkage and breakage.[112] Wrigley complied and the revised claim with a supporting statement from Junior Chief Trader Edmund Beeston, chief accountant for the Northern Department, was forwarded to Ottawa in late December.[113]

The Royal Commission on Rebellion Losses Claims chaired by J. Alphonse Ouimette, a Montreal lawyer, was scheduled to meet at Battleford at the end of February and Wrigley was hopeful that all claims would be settled by the end of the year. The company's claim was heard in late April 1886. The commission's first report, issued on 28 May 1887, dashed Wrigley's hopes for a speedy settlement. It found that amounts claimed for fur losses as well as those charged for flour, country produce and buildings destroyed by fire at Carlton, were excessive and concluded with the following recommendations:

TABLE 1   HBC Rebellion Losses Claims

	Claimed	Allowed
Carlton	$ 53,342.38	$ 48,057.13
Battleford	22,969.61	22,929.64
Fort Pitt	39,321.99	35,870.91
Lac la Biche	9,798.38	8,717.78
Battle River Crossing	1,770.15	1,765.72
Green Lake	45,840.50	45,808.50
25.5% surcharge	34,072.83	0.00
Supplementary Claims	2,328.03	618.91
TOTAL CLAIM	209,443.87	163,768.59

(Source: HBCA, E.9/30, fo. 104)

---

[111]HBCA, D.13/7, fo. 281, Wrigley to Armit, 4 November 1885.

[112]Average transit time from London to the post was eighteen months.

[113]NAC, *Department of the Interior*, vol. 532, file 154289, 30 December 1885.

A cheque for the final amount was subsequently mailed to Wrigley on 1 August.[114] The company was not the only concern to have its claim reduced. The CPR claim was cut by $114,713; the Winnipeg and Western Navigation (Transportation) Company by $17,970; the Northwestern [North West] Navigation Company by $11,651.50; North-West Coal and Navigation Company by $17,804; and W.R. Sinclair, freighter, by $11,530.[115]

The commission stated that although the company had charged London prices minus insurance and shipping for its furs, it could only allow the same price as those lost by other claimants which was the purchase price of the furs at the various places where they were pillaged. The commission rejected the additional charge of 25.5 per cent, stating that prices charged in the claim were ample to cover all expenditures associated with these goods.

Wrigley's response was quick. He refuted the commission's fur pricing system on the grounds that there was no local market worth mentioning at Battleford, Fort Pitt, Lac la Biche or Battle River Crossing. In addressing the question of the 25.5 per cent surtax, Wrigley referred to sworn evidence by Beeston proving that the company had paid this money, which did not include allowance for profit or consequential damage. If the company was not reimbursed it would be a loser to that extent.

Turning to the supplementary claims which had been disallowed, including the furnishing of supplies to Indians and loyal settlers, Wrigley pointed out that the Indian Department had acknowledged the justness of the company's claim and repaid a portion. However that department was not authorized to pay for supplies to other than Indians. The company's actions had undoubtedly prevented a number of Métis from joining the rebellion. It was under this conviction that the Indian Department had paid its portion of the claim and Wrigley expressed the hope that the company would not be asked to bear the remaining expense.[116]

Wrigley filed a supplementary claim with the commission for $1,694.76 of which $1,369.32 was allowed.[117] He refused to acknowledge this payment as a complete settlement although he admitted to Armit that he had not much hope of obtaining more. Over the next three years he continued to importune the Minister of the Interior but his arguments fell on deaf ears. The ministry closed the file in 1890, stating that after careful consideration it did not feel justified in revising its decision.

Other urgent matters demanded much speedier resolution. At the close of the rebellion, the company's transportation system was in disarray. Entire northern outfits,

---

[114]HBCA, A.12/53, fo. 275a, cable, Donald A. Smith to London, 3 August 1887.

[115]*The Commercial*, 7 December 1886.

[116]NAC, *Department of the Interior*, vol. 532, file 154289, Wrigley to White, 9 September 1887.

[117]Ibid., file 182410, copy of a Report of a Committee of the Privy Council, 11 July 1888.

on which the forthcoming year's trade and sustenance were dependent, had been destroyed and the region between the northwestern posts and headquarters was still in a state of unease. As the company approached the beginning of a new outfit, its financial picture was bleak. Its claims with the government totalled over $209,000 of which $45,675 would never be paid. By 1885, charges for taxes and surveys coupled with shareholders' dividends had eaten up all the profits leaving a balance on hand in the land department account of £12.[118]

Economic depression was worsening throughout the North West with disastrous effects on the company's land values and general trade. With the consequent decline in purchasing power, cancellations of land sales escalated. Instead of promoting sales, the land department concentrated on collecting arrears, with less than satisfactory results. As funds dried up, demand for consumer goods declined. Numerous bankruptcies flooded the market with cut rate stock which cut profit margins even further. Immigration, and with it future markets for the company's retail trade, declined drastically. The board had long recognized the need for a thorough reorganization of its general trade, which was one of the major reasons Wrigley had been hired, but the rebellion had delayed any concrete steps in this area. Citing a 72 per cent drop in profits from the previous year due to a 40-50 per cent decline in fur prices and uncertain how long its capital would be tied up by the costs of the rebellion, the board declined to issue a dividend for 1885. Given the current economic situation no immediate profits could be expected from either land or general trade. Therefore the company had no choice but to turn to its traditional mainstay, the fur trade, to sustain it through the crisis.

---

[118]HBC, *Proceedings*, 30 June 1885, p. 7.

Chapter 3

SHORING UP THE FOUNDATION:
MODERNIZING THE FUR TRADE

In taking on the supervision of the fur trade, Wrigley was at a distinct disadvantage. Armed with no more background than that provided by a brief orientation session, he had arrived in Winnipeg in 1884 with a mandate to reorganize the company's trade in accordance with modern business principles. He joined an organization steeped in over two centuries of tradition run by men who, in most instances, had spent all their adult lives in the trade. United by common interests and often by family ties with roots in the Scottish Highlands and Orkney Islands,[119] the commissioned officers were proud, independent men accustomed to making personal decisions regarding their own districts. They viewed themselves, rightly, as the backbone of the company's North American trading operations and resisted any move on the part of the board to reorganize.

As Donald A. Smith had anticipated, the announcement of the trade commissioner's appointment prompted rumblings of discontent from several of the senior and most influential officers.[120] Despite their failings, Wrigley's predecessors, Smith and Grahame, had earned the respect of fellow officers throughout the service for their years spent actively involved in the fur trade, each man rising steadily through the ranks to his appointment as chief commissioner.[121] Wrigley, on the other hand, was an outsider who would have to prove himself.

Inefficiencies in the supply system had been of less concern prior to 1870 when the company enjoyed a monopoly throughout most of Rupert's Land. In addition to the chronic problem of transportation delays, the company's accounting procedures were too rudimentary to indicate how individual districts or posts were doing at any given time. Although the Canadian subcommittee had been established in May 1884 to provide closer control over operations, it was concerned primarily with the land department. However, as the west opened up and competition for diminishing resources increased, the board

---

[119]National differences formed a strong undercurrent in relations between officers and management. Commenting on the promotion of Edmund K. Beeston, Chief Factor Peter W. Bell wrote: "These dd Englishmen are simply having their own way - if kept in my dear fellow for a few years longer Scotchmen and their forebears will be a thing of the past." NAC, *MacFarlane Papers*, fo. 1276, Bell to Roderick MacFarlane, 28 September 1890.

[120]NAC, *Sandford Fleming Papers*, vol. 48, folder 331, Smith to Fleming, 19 August 1884.

[121]At the time they assumed this position, Grahame had accumulated 32 years of service in the Northern and Western Departments and Smith had served 34 years in the Montreal and Northern Departments.

finally acknowledged that major changes were needed if the fur trade was to remain viable.

Wrigley immediately set to work to reorganize the system of indenting. At that time each geographic department operated autonomously, indenting and corresponding directly with London. It was common practice to order goods from London up to two years in advance to allow for transportation time. Under this system the amount of unsaleable stock on hand at individual posts was always a problem as it was impossible to predict requirements with any accuracy that far in advance.

As a first step, Wrigley recommended that part of the new Winnipeg store be designated as a supply depot for the Northern Department. Samples and patterns would be sent out to individual posts from which officers could make selections. Orders would then be forwarded to the commissioner and subcommittee for approval and filled by the depot buyers. Goods would be shipped to northern posts at the Winnipeg cost-landed price which would include half of all depot salaries and costs. The depot would not recoup all its costs, but Wrigley hoped the new system would quell the common misconception among northern officers that the Winnipeg store was making a profit on goods shipped to them.

Although the board approved in principle of Wrigley's proposal, it expressed concern that the new system of indenting through the depot would incur extra expense. Wrigley persisted and the board finally relented, inaugurating the new system in February 1885. Old habits died hard, however, as Wrigley questioned time and again why large orders were being forwarded from posts which received daily rail service.[122]

Wrigley turned his attention next to the Western Department which, according to Chief Factor William Charles' annual report, was in a very unsatisfactory state. The arrival of the Northern Pacific Railway in Portland, Oregon in 1883 had permanently changed the nature of the business and future prospects were dim. Independent traders were quick to capitalize on the railway and telegraph to relay supplies and money. With increased competition for furs and an expanding cash trade it became increasingly difficult for the company to maintain profit levels. Wrigley advised the board against closing posts. Rather, he urged that the company should adapt to altered circumstances and make vigorous efforts to increase both its general business in the south and the collection of furs in the north. Without more firsthand information, Wrigley was wary of making major changes, but he reassured the board that, once the transcontinental railway was completed, many parts of the Western Department would be better served by rail through Winnipeg rather than by clipper ship via Cape Horn or the Isthmus of Panama.[123]

---

[122]HBCA, D.14/9, fo. 239, Wrigley to Alex Matheson, Rat Portage, 30 September 1885 and fo. 243, Wrigley to Archibald McDonald, Fort Qu'Appelle, 30 September 1885.

[123]These voyages usually took six months, leaving London in December and arriving at Victoria in June.

As a first step in reorganization, Wrigley proposed the creation of a two-man inspection team consisting of one member familiar with the fur trade and the other with modern principles of retail trade. Following the model of bank inspectors, the team would travel to any trading district or post. In devising the system, Wrigley placed great emphasis on not weakening the authority of district officers. The former position of Inspecting Chief Factor had been a superior rank and was often the source of jealousy and suspicion. Now, inspection officers would report directly to the commissioner and recommendations would be made through him rather than through subordinate officers against whom an appeal could be filed. Wrigley introduced the title Inspecting Officer which carried no additional rank and was a salaried position rather than one based on an apportionment of shares.

The board agreed to a continuous system of inspection the following April (1885), focusing on the supply, sale and inventory of goods as well as general operations and trade prospects in each district. To provide a basis for comparison, the board asked Wrigley to supply a list of trading districts, inventories and a complete financial statement for the past three years. Chief Factor Peter W. Bell was appointed the first acting inspector in June 1886 but he was discharged from his inspection duties shortly thereafter for drunkenness. Junior Chief Trader Edmund K. Beeston, chief accountant at Winnipeg, carried on with some difficulty, as he lacked familiarity with the fur trade, until he was joined in 1888 by Chief Factor Richard Hardisty, an experienced officer in charge of the Upper Saskatchewan District.[124]

At the same time that it approved the inspection system, the board moved to reorganize the Western Department by granting a leave of absence to Chief Factor William Charles preparatory to his resignation at the close of Trading Year '85. Charles had foreseen his fate in a letter to Chief Factor Roderick MacFarlane earlier that year:

> Well I have been expecting catastrophes for some time and expect they are not far off. I am personally unknown to all the members of the Board, to D.A. Smith and the officers on the other side & when they want to "reorganize" the Western Department, off will go my head to make room perhaps, either for a relative, a protege or a modern man, up to snuff.[125]

---

[124]Richard Hardisty, brother-in-law of Donald A. Smith, joined the company in 1849 as an apprentice post master in the Red River District. He served at a number of posts in the Northern Department until 1872 when he was made Chief Factor and appointed to the charge of the Upper Saskatchewan District, headquartered in Edmonton, where he remained for 17 years. He ran unsuccessfully as an independent candidate in the first general election for the District of Alberta in 1887 and in 1888, in addition to his appointment as acting inspector, he was called to the Senate (Shirlee Ann Smith, "Richard Hardisty" in *DCB*, vol. XI, pp. 383-384).

[125]NAC, *MacFarlane Papers*, fo. 1038, Charles to MacFarlane, 21 February 1885,

(continued...)

Chief Factor Alex Munro assumed command until T.R. Smith, the company's assistant secretary, could be transferred from his temporary assignment in the Red River District to the new post of assistant trade commissioner in charge of the Western Department. Upon Smith's appointment, a new system was inaugurated whereby copies of all of his correspondence as well as Western Department officers' reports were forwarded to Wrigley for instructions. Wrigley also received copies of their London outward correspondence to keep him apprised of department affairs.

In an attempt to define his own position more clearly, Wrigley questioned whether the Western, Montreal and Southern Departments should remain semi-independent with the trade commissioner little more than the nominal head or, like the Northern Department, be brought under his direct control. He urged a policy of fixed responsibilities with a clear cut chain of command from the board to the commissioned officers through the commissioner. With greater centralization, he argued, capital expenditures could be better controlled and the wishes of the board could be more easily carried out. The proposed new inspection system would be of great assistance in this regard enabling Wrigley to keep his finger on the pulse of each district.[126]

His first attempts to consolidate authority were unsuccessful. While the board generally agreed with his argument that officers should be responsible to the commissioner as laid down in the Deed Poll, owing to the difficulties in communication and the nature of the business, a certain amount of authority had to be vested in the officers and it was important that their authority in matters pertaining to trade and discipline in the service not be weakened. Wrigley's attempts to persuade Chief Factor Samuel K. Parsons, head of the Montreal Department, to indent through the commissioner's office rather than directly on London met with a similar fate and he had to be content with having the subcommittee assume that responsibility.[127]

Another integral part of the fur trade that came under Wrigley's jurisdiction was the northern transportation system. Chief Factor Julian Camsell of Port Simpson visited Wrigley in December 1884 and endorsed Chief Factor Roderick MacFarlane's urgent request for a steamer on the Mackenzie River, an idea which had received Donald A. Smith's enthusiastic support.[128] The potential benefits were numerous. With a more reliable and efficient mode of transportation to the Mackenzie River and Athabaska districts, a year's shipping time would be saved, costs halved, indenting reduced and

---

[125](...continued)
private. Charles lost his ties to the commissioner's office when James A. Grahame resigned in 1884. Grahame's first wife, Birnie, was a sister of Mrs. Charles. (*Victoria Daily Colonist*, 29 April 1951, p. 11).

[126]HBCA, D.13/7, fos. 193d-194, Wrigley to Armit, 18 May 1885.

[127]HBCA, D.14/9, fos. 288-289d, Wrigley to Parsons, 9 November 1885.

[128]NAC, *MacFarlane Papers*, fo. 997, Donald A. Smith to MacFarlane, 25 November 1884.

opposition effectively wiped out along the 1200 miles to the Arctic coast. Ideally, northern outfits could be shipped from England in the spring, carried by rail to Calgary, then carted overland to the steamer at Athabaska Landing. If this could be accomplished by the first of June, outfits would reach their destination within the same shipping year. The entire system, Wrigley estimated, would save the company $2500 annually.[129]

The board authorized the construction of the Mackenzie River steamer in February 1885. Captain John M. Smith, who had built the *Grahame*, was sent to Athabaska Landing to superintend the transport of machinery to Fort McMurray. From here the *Grahame* would carry the cargo to Fort Smith where the steamer would be built to meet the 1 June 1886 deadline. Wrigley authorized Chief Factor Richard Hardisty to repair the road between Edmonton and Athabaska Landing and plans were made to test the new route with some of the Northern Department outfits while the remainder would be sent by the traditional Portage la Loche route.

At the same time, with the imminent completion of the transcontinental railway, the company recognized it was about to lose exclusive control over the transportation of its trade goods. The new rail line was the key to transportation reorganization and the question of freight rates was urgent. The company's only recourse was to negotiate a special arrangement with the CPR. In the company's favour was the size of its shipments, the distance involved and, not least, the fact that one of their major shareholders and Canadian subcommittee member Donald A. Smith was a member of the railway syndicate.

In February 1885 Wrigley had initial discussions in Montreal with William Van Horne, General Traffic Manager of the CPR. The railway proposed a discount of 10 per cent on current rates over the entire system to offset National Policy tariffs, as well as a special rebate east of Winnipeg in return for a CPR monopoly on shipping wherever possible. Furs were excluded, however, because of their high value and perishability. Also exempt were grain and flour since current rates in the railway's western division already placed the company in a favourable position in relation to other millers who had invested substantial money in their operations.[130]

These exclusions weighed heavily on the company's two major sources of export revenue. Wrigley's counterproposal for a 15 per cent rebate was based on the argument that current freight rates already included risk to furs. In addition, if the Hudson's Bay Company accepted a CPR monopoly, it would be subject to restrictions not faced by other millers. A discount of 12.5 per cent on all freight except flour was finally negotiated but it was a fragile agreement. After not receiving the usual rebate one week, Wrigley learned informally that the CPR was "much put out" by what it perceived to be an unfriendly attitude on the part of T.R. Smith of Victoria and Chief Factor Samuel

---

[129]HBCA, D.13/7, fo. 103, Wrigley to Armit, 12 January 1885.

[130]HBCA, D.13/7, n.f., Robert Kerr, CPR general freight agent, to Wrigley, 14 April 1885. For a more detailed account of the company's milling operations, see Chapter IV.

Parsons, head of the Montreal Department. He warned both officers that, considering the connection that must exist between the two companies, it was absolutely necessary that they remain on good terms even though the company might not always get its due.[131]

The company needed all the financial assistance it could get. The results of the March 1885 fur sales were disastrous with fur prices declining 40-50 per cent over the previous year. This was blamed on the general depression, with a consequent drop in purchasing power and less demand for luxury furs. With profits plummeting from £110,000 in 1884 to £20,000, the board declined to pay a dividend. On the recommendation of the Canadian subcommittee, it also proposed reducing the tariff on which cash prices of furs were based by one third. The board anticipated that fewer furs would be taken as a result but hoped that it would not have an adverse effect at sales shops where goods rather than cash were often exchanged for furs.[132] Wrigley argued that prime furs could not be purchased at two thirds valuation and that a reassessment of this policy was urgently needed. Independent traders were moving in and the company was losing control of the market. The board sanctioned a 10 per cent increase but stressed that goods be given in preference to cash advances. In distant northern districts, however, opposition traders were allowed to take the furs rather than have the company suffer a loss.

A constant problem was that small traders appeared much better informed than HBC officers on fur prices as well as the condition and prospects of the market. For example, although results of the March 1885 sale were cabled to Wrigley, the figures were known in Winnipeg two or three days before the telegram arrived. As a result, large quantities of prime furs were snapped up at lower prices by the competition. Wrigley suggested, as a first step, that current information on price fluctuations be telegraphed more frequently and the tariff updated periodically. He warned the board that in the case of a price decline, uninformed officers would be paying too much and incur even greater losses. Conversely, a low tariff based on a poor March sale could be followed by a rise in the market. Officers would be unable to adjust their prices with the result that furs would go to traders who were not tied to a fixed tariff.[133]

The board was not convinced. Although independent traders might correctly anticipate market fluctuations from time to time, it was confident that the only safe guide

---

[131]HBCA, D.14/10, fo. 689, Wrigley to T.R. Smith, private, 15 March 1887.

[132]It was company policy to pay more for furs obtained through barter as opposed to cash as it was more profitable (A.J. Ray, *The Canadian Fur Trade in the Industrial Age*, pp. 76-77).

[133]When setting its tariff, the company also had to take into account the cost of maintaining its Canadian network of posts which independent traders did not (A.J. Ray, "Marketing Canadian Furs, 1870-1945: A Preliminary Discussion", p. 2).

in setting the annual tariff was the spring sale results.[134] It was not until 1887 that Wrigley's persistent demands for current information finally paid off. During that year's January sale, news of a rise in beaver prices was cabled to him, giving the company a few hours' head start and several lots of fur were purchased at a trifle over the old prices.[135]

During August 1885 Wrigley visited the Saskatchewan River District to assess the effects of the North West Rebellion, travelling by rail to Calgary, overland to Edmonton, then back by boat. Upon his return, he embarked on a series of staff cuts in the district's more unprofitable areas. Rather than close posts, Wrigley preferred to change management and initiated a series of transfers that autumn while forwarding letters of warning to other post officers.

His report to the board was not optimistic. Many fur trade posts had suffered damage, either from troop occupation or raids. Several posts were poorly located and capital was needed to upgrade others along Lake Winnipeg. Indian debt was a growing concern. Wrigley favoured its discontinuance in frontier areas, since Indians often preferred to spend their treaty money where they could get full value, rather than where some of it was owed to the company. Consequently, the company lost both the debt and the furs.[136] He had met with band chiefs at various posts and remarked that they seemed anxious to trade and to maintain good relations with HBC officers. Their situation would be less difficult, he concluded, if government officials treated them as well as company officers did.

That October, Wrigley made his much postponed visit to the Western Department. He found the company's business generally unsatisfactory and laid much of the blame on the senior officer Chief Factor William Charles.[137] Posts had been closed unwisely. Discipline was lacking throughout the entire department and officers did not appear to understand their duties. Fur supplies were dwindling and, given the small population, a large increase in trade was unlikely, although the mining industry was anticipated to have a positive effect at Yale, Hope and Langley. Most of the capital had been invested in Victoria where the retail business was very small, the emphasis being placed on its wholesale trade.[138] Stock on hand and outstanding debts were excessive, a problem not uncommon to the wholesale trade. The completion of the CPR would remedy the stock problem and Wrigley hoped that any increase in freight rates would be offset by interest

---

[134]For a description of the various fur fairs which were held in London and Europe see Henry Poland, *Fur Bearing Animals in Nature and In Commerce*, pp. liv-lvi.

[135]HBCA, D.13/8, fo. 144d, Wrigley to Armit, 31 January 1887.

[136]HBCA, D.14/9, fos. 191d-192, Wrigley to P.W. Bell, 16 September 1885.

[137]HBCA, D.13/7, fos. 272-279, Wrigley to Armit, 26 October 1885.

[138]A detailed description of the company's wholesale trade facilities appears in *The Commercial*, 27 August 1888.

saved on the six-month sea voyage. Towards this end, Wrigley recommended one central depot for both Northern and Western Departments and the purchase of Canadian goods by tender, in his opinion the best and safest mode of buying.

In an effort to expand operations into previously untapped areas, Wrigley asked Chief Factor James McDougall to visit the area north of New Caledonia between Alaska and the Mackenzie River District and to report on the most economical means of obtaining furs which were currently being siphoned off by American fur traders. As a result of his report, Wrigley authorized the establishment of a new post in the vicinity of the Dease, Liard and Nahanni Rivers to halt the advance of their main opponent, Sylvester, and made the first of several recommendations for a small steamer for the Stikeen River. The board was not enthusiastic, fearing that such a move would open up the region to further competition.

By November the yearly indents for England were arriving and Wrigley took the opportunity to further reduce inventory by encouraging those districts which could indent twice a year to do so. He also asked the board if contracts for goods supplied on a yearly basis could have the quantities left open as was normally done in government and English railway tenders. This would allow officers the maximum time possible to fix quantities and the company would not have to pay for the goods until they were actually required.

The board gave Wrigley full authority to act in this regard and the success of the new system was evident by January 1886 when Wrigley forwarded the Northern Department indent noting that it had decreased by £13,342 over the previous year.[139] The board's confidence in Wrigley was reflected in the rosy picture it painted for shareholders at the annual December meeting. Donald A. Smith praised Wrigley's efforts on the company's behalf as those of a gentleman who "although not formerly connected with the business, has given himself with such assiduity and ability to it, that I believe he will be able to give you a good account both of the commercial business and the fur trade from year to year."[140]

His hopes appeared to be well founded. By the spring of 1886 fur market prospects had improved moderately due to a fashion trend away from dyed skins to the rich natural colours of luxury furs. Beaver, otter and mink were in high demand resulting in a 28 per cent advance in fur prices at the annual spring sale.[141]

The company's northernmost transportation system appeared to be flourishing as well. In May 1886, Chief Factor Julian Camsell reported that steady progress was being made on the Mackenzie River steamer, to be named the *Wrigley*. In addition, a warehouse, store and other buildings were also being constructed at Athabaska Landing to serve as a depot for northern trade.

---

[139]HBCA, D.13/7, fo. 330, Wrigley to Armit, 11 January 1886.

[140]HBC, *Proceedings*, 15 December 1885, p. 8.

[141]*The Commercial*, 18 May 1886.

Other areas were beset by chronic problems. That summer, transportation was halted on the Saskatchewan River system due to low water levels which made it impossible for the *Northwest* and the *Northcote* to pass the cut-off at Cumberland. While this did not affect northern outfits which had been shipped earlier, goods required for Indian Department and North West Mounted Police contracts were stranded and had to be duplicated and shipped overland at considerable expense. Low water levels plagued shipping on the Saskatchewan for the rest of the decade and by 1890 only the *Northwest* was in operation. The opening of branch rail lines to Prince Albert did away with the Grand Rapids route and when the *Northcote* required repairs, the owners declined to advance the necessary funds due to the low volume of business.[142]

As 1886 drew to a close, Wrigley could reflect on the success of major changes to the company's general supply system. For the first time, Western Department furs had been shipped east by rail and favourable freight rates to Vancouver encouraged Wrigley to open a temporary establishment there under the direction of Factor William Livock, formerly of the Victoria depot. The wreck of the *Cam Owen* that autumn off Cape Churchill, with the loss of its cargo destined for Churchill, York Factory and surrounding areas, would have been a disaster in previous years when all Northern Department indents were funnelled through York Factory. Now, although its loss would create problems in transporting the next year's returns to London, the board was able to assure shareholders that it would not seriously affect the trade.[143]

Prospects appeared less rosy for the commissioned officers. The annual guarantee of £200 per share was due to expire at the end of Trading Year '84 and Wrigley petitioned the board for a permanent arrangement or, at least, renewal for another term. The board agreed to put the matter before the shareholders at the next annual meeting. Unwilling to wait, Chief Factor Roderick MacFarlane, a senior officer recently in charge of the Athabaska District, took advantage of a year's furlough to meet with Governor Colvile and board member Lord Anson in London to discuss officers' concerns.[144] He defended his right to represent them in a letter to Deputy Governor Sir John Rose, requesting that a pension fund be established to provide officers with some financial security.[145]

---

[142]HBCA, F.36/1, n.f., *13th Annual Report, Winnipeg and Western Transportation Company*, 28 February 1891.

[143]HBC, *Proceedings*, 7 December 1886.

[144]Roderick MacFarlane entered the service in 1852 and spent many years in the Mackenzie River District. He was active in the negotiations leading to the Deed Poll of 1871 and throughout his years of service he built up a wide network of friends throughout the fur trade who were regular correspondents.

[145]NAC, *MacFarlane Papers*, fo. 1060, MacFarlane to Deputy Governor Sir John Rose, 29 April 1886. Prior to the passage of the British Old Age Pensions Bill in 1908, pensions were the responsibility of individual employers.

On being informed of MacFarlane's actions, Wrigley reassured the board that a little tact and firmness would be sufficient to handle the situation. The officers' grievances, he felt, were based on pride in their role as both officers and partners. The tariff on officers' and clerks' supplies had recently been raised without prior consultation by as much as 60 per cent for those living at posts beyond the reach of the railway. As a result they naturally felt that their position was being downgraded to little better than that of company servants.

The board was not very receptive. MacFarlane was granted a leave of absence for the remainder of the outfit whereupon he would be served notice of termination to take effect 1 June 1887.[146] Wrigley was quickly approached by Lawrence Clarke, head of the Saskatchewan District, to intercede on MacFarlane's behalf.[147] A letter signed by Chief Factors Alex Munro of Victoria, Clarke and Richard Hardisty of Edmonton reminded Wrigley of MacFarlane's many years of service and of his assignment as head of one of the most important districts where he had uniformly shown large returns and good profits at the expense of both his health and financial situation.

But their letter was more than a plea on MacFarlane's behalf. They went on to give a frank assessment of the existing sentiment among officers in the service. They rejected the common misconception among shareholders that increased settlement had a detrimental effect on the fur trade. In fact, over the past five years, fur returns in all districts, with the exception of Red River, compared favourably with the period prior to the arrival of the CPR despite the fact that the railway had brought competition to all branches of the business. The company's commissioned officers were trained in the fur trade and it constituted their sole means of support. Where a share once averaged £250 before reorganization, it was currently worth only £200. Now officers who would have gladly retired from the company in good feeling were forced to struggle on, "afraid as they are, to leave and risk starvation in their old age."[148] If they were left at retirement with insufficient funds they would have no recourse but to fall back on trading in direct competition with the company. Although they assured the board that this was not to be interpreted as a threat, it was exactly that.

The letter came at an opportune time. Wrigley had already brought to the board's attention the small number of officers who were familiar with the company's commercial operations, a major stumbling block if it hoped to expand in this area. He concluded that there were too many officers and suggested that a small pension fund be set up to provide a tangible incentive to retire and stimulate the flow of promotions. Now it appeared that rather than having to face a wall of opposition from the officers they had, on their own, put forward an identical proposal albeit from different motives.

---

[146]HBCA, A.1/153, fo. 96, 13 July 1886.

[147]Wrigley had developed a strong friendship with Clarke and lengthy private letters often accompanied their official correspondence.

[148]GI, *Richard Hardisty Papers*, box 8, file 259, fo. 1697, Munro to Wrigley, 9 August 1886. Draft copy.

Consequently, the board passed a resolution limiting the number of officers to 50 and Wrigley and the subcommittee were canvassed to determine how this could best be accomplished. Wrigley recommended that the board extend the minimum guarantee of £200 per share to unappropriated shares for a fixed period of time. These funds, combined with the Fur Trade Officers Reserve Fund,[149] could be used to finance the pension. He proposed that an annuity of £100 to £250 be granted over a period of five to seven years. Pensioners would be allowed to engage in any trade as long as there was no direct or indirect interest in the fur trade. He included a list of candidates for retirement and suggested, as well, that a number of clerks could be dispensed with in the same manner if a similar fund could be established.[150]

This did not deter MacFarlane from his personal crusade and he again travelled to London to address the annual shareholders' meeting. He arrived on 11 December 1886 only to find that the board, forewarned by Donald A. Smith, had convened the meeting four days earlier. But support for his reinstatement was slowly building throughout the Northern Department and, as in the past, the united opposition of the commissioned officers was effective. Fearing that he would join the opposition upon termination and not wishing to alienate the officers further, the board backed down and reinstated him, not to the prestigious Athabaska District but to the more remote New Caledonia. Officers were assured that the proposed new pension plan, set up along guidelines proposed by Wrigley, would be put to the shareholders at the next meeting. Although allocations from the fund would continue to be made at the disposition of the board, officers would be entitled to make recommendations. Once the requisite number of shares had been freed up by retirements, the board would consider promotions of company clerks to officer rank.

In introducing the pension plan to the shareholders, the board assured them that it would not interfere with the efficiency of the service nor make any fresh demands on their pockets. Appeased by a 17 shilling per share dividend, the shareholders gave the scheme their unanimous approval and voted to continue the annual guarantee which would remain in effect until 1893.[151]

The board then proceeded to select six men for retirement stating that if they did not resign after receiving Wrigley's communication, formal notice would be given. By May the resignations of two factors, two chief traders and one junior chief trader had been accepted with another junior chief trader following suit two months later. The following year the board prepared a list of commissioned officers in each department with the actual number of men considered sufficient to carry on the trade. It concluded that an additional ten officers could be dropped from the service without injury to the

---

[149]The Officers Reserve Fund had been established by the terms of the Deed Poll of 1871 for the benefit of officers and/or their families.

[150]HBCA, D.13/8, fos. 100d-102d, Wrigley to Armit, 9 November 1886.

[151]HBC, *Report*, p. 5, 18 June 1887.

TABLE 2   PAYMENTS TO COMMISSIONED OFFICERS, 1885-1894

Year	Trading Year	Officers' Share of Profits	HBC Contribution to Guarantee	Total
1885	1883	Nil	£19,200	£19,200
1886	1884	£10,242	9,658	19,900
1887	1885	30,714	Nil	30,714
1888	1886	Nil	19,500	19,500
1889	1887	17,371	2,429	19,800
1890	1888	Nil	19,800	19,800
1891	1889	Nil	19,800	19,600
1892	1890	Nil	18,880	18,880
1893	1891	8,866	9,254	18,120
1894	1892	4,423	13,697	18,120

(Source: HBC, *Report* for each fiscal year as cited in
Oleson, "Commissioned Officers", p. 242)

trade and Wrigley was instructed to contact six more officers and secure their resignations.[152]

At the same time, the board noted that many of the Standing Rules and Regulations revised by Commissioner Grahame in 1877 had become obsolete.[153] Wrigley had worked steadily during the previous year drafting revisions and had forwarded a new list to the board in January 1887 for their approval. After some modifications, made at the board's request, the final draft was circulated to every factor and chief factor for consideration before a Council of the commissioned officers was called in August 1888.

Much remained to be done in the meantime. After examining the company's pricing system, Wrigley questioned the policy of setting an average value for the same species of fur regardless of quality. Officers' promotions were based on apparent rather than actual value of the district or post they commanded; consequently they often placed greater emphasis on obtaining furs of inferior quality which were in greater supply. Realizing this, Indian traders offered common skins to the company and reserved prime pelts for the opposition where they would command a better price. With everything

---

[152]According to the terms of the Deed Poll, no more than seven officers could retire in one year.

[153]The majority of the regulations were established in 1843 and added to by each annual council thereafter as new exigencies arose.

based on quantity it was impossible to determine accurately how each department was actually doing. To remedy this, Wrigley recommended that a record be kept by district of the various grades of fur when they were sorted in the London warehouse. After a sale, the average valuation for each grade would be calculated, and from this, the actual value of each department's balance sheet determined.[154]

After some consideration, the board responded that separate valuations of prime and common skins would not assist officers in regulating their purchases. The only reliable guides were the sales catalogues which classified each district's returns and listed the actual sale price.[155] Valuations were then calculated by deducting 20 per cent to cover expenses and profit. However, Wrigley was authorized to allow officers to exceed the tariff rate for prime skins.[156] In a separate report, board member Edward Harris vetoed Wrigley's proposal to value each post's returns by separate assortment citing the extra expense and time that such a method would entail.[157]

In the spring of 1887, news from the northern districts was gloomy. Peace River, English River and Athabaska Districts all reported outbreaks of measles which ravaged the Indians. Wrigley had written to Lawrence Vankoughnet, Deputy Superintendent General of Indian Affairs, earlier in the year regarding the northern Indians' plight only to receive the reply that only the Prime Minister could make decisions in this area and he was presently engaged in electioneering. Wrigley then met with Vankoughnet during his annual visit to the Montreal Department and "spoke very strongly on the absolute necessity of action as human life was even of more importance than electioneering."[158] Consequently, Wrigley received permission from the Government to furnish all necessary aid to treaty Indians and, if absolutely necessary, non-treaty Indians.

Game was scarce and the shift to imported provisions placed even greater strain on the company's resources. Despite the advantages of an improved transportation system and prestige built up over many years, the company bore the heavy expense of maintaining northern posts and supporting large numbers of servants and labourers.[159]

---

[154]HBCA, D.13/8, fos. 105d-108d, Wrigley to Armit, 9 November 1886.

[155]At this time there was nothing to identify furs from a particular post as only district marks were used on the packs.

[156]Between 30 March and 28 April 1887, 16 authorizations were given in the Montreal, Western and Northern Departments.

[157]HBCA, D.19/14, n.f., extract from board minutes, 11 January 1887, enclosure in letter from Armit to Wrigley of the same date.

[158]HBCA, D.13/8, fo. 166d, Wrigley to Armit, 14 March 1887.

[159]There were 70 servants at Fort Chipewyan alone at an estimated cost to the company of £25 per annum (HBCA, D.13/8, fo. 259d, Wrigley to Armit, 27 August 1887). Often the company was forced to provide extended employment to native

(continued...)

Independent traders specialized in imported goods and a wide range of popular novelties which were easily transported leaving the company to supply heavy and less profitable staples such as flour, bacon and blankets.

Morale among the company's men dipped lower as competition reached as far north as Port Simpson and traders outflanked the company by purchasing a schooner to tap the Queen Charlotte Islands. Early in 1887 Wrigley learned that the company's main opponent in New Caledonia, Sylvester, was considering retirement. Usually, Wrigley supported company policy of not buying out the competition but in this case, he argued successfully that an exception be made as New Caledonia was rich in furs and important to the protection of the adjacent Mackenzie River [Cassiar] District, the only district free of traders.

Attacks were also being made on other fronts. Americans trading in Hudson Bay paid no import duty on their goods, placing company posts at a distinct disadvantage. The problem had been raised in Ottawa but the government declined to underwrite the expense of sending a Revenue cutter north, leaving the company to fend for itself.

That spring (1887) Wrigley set off on a two-month tour of the troubled Northern Department. Injecting a rare personal note into his correspondence, he admitted his anxiety about proving a good traveller but he assured the board that he would do his best as the visit was very desirable.[160] His report only confirmed those of previous years. Competition was strong in all areas and native people, perceiving the company as timid and dependent, were making increased demands that had been acceded to for fear of losing their trade. Indian debts had been authorized and cancelled without discretion leaving the door open to dishonesty. Administrative reorganization coupled with a new Indian policy was badly needed. After conferring with officers, Wrigley was convinced that abolishing the Indian debt system was the right course to pursue. He cautioned that changes would have to be introduced gradually and that necessities such as ammunition would still have to be advanced. The transition would be difficult but he had every confidence that the result would offset increases in fur tariffs which the company needed to remain competitive.

The decline in fur bearers, particularly beaver, was a major problem. There was no closed season and the young were being ruthlessly killed. Law enforcement was difficult in remote districts and, although the officers did their best, in the face of increased competition the situation was almost hopeless. Donald A. Smith, when approached, did not think it advisable to establish closed seasons as this might introduce officials from outside the company into more remote districts.[161]

---

[159](...continued)
labourers to ensure that they were available when they were most needed (A.J. Ray, "The Decline of Paternalism in the HBC Fur Trade", p. 195).

[160]On this journey north to Port Simpson the *Wrigley* became the first steamer to cross the Arctic Circle (*Edmonton Bulletin*, 20 August 1887).

[161]HBCA, D.49/1, fo. 244d, Smith to Armit, 28 October 1887.

The Western Department was little better. Although T.R. Smith appeared to have a firm grasp on commercial operations, he lacked a thorough understanding of the fur trade and no one in Victoria could give him much assistance. The wholesale business often conflicted with inland trade and the charge that the Victoria Sales Shop showed more promptness and care in executing competitor's orders than those of company posts was not unfounded. At this point Wrigley said nothing to discourage Smith's enthusiasm, confident that, given time, he would succeed.

Improvements had been made to the Thompson River District by ordering goods by the carload wherever possible and the reassignment of Roderick MacFarlane to New Caledonia was an attempt to remedy the deplorable condition to which it had sunk under former management. In order to cut overland transportation costs, Wrigley again requested a small steamer to serve the Skeena and Stikine River area. The board remained unenthusiastic. While isolation was a major contributor to transportation costs, it also protected HBC posts from competitors who did not hesitate to take advantage of any new routes into the interior.

After a year's deliberation, the commissioned officers met in council in Winnipeg to deal with the proposed new rules and regulations for the trade. The August 1888 meeting at the Queen Hotel was an historic event for, unknown to the participants, it would be the last council of the commissioned officers of the Hudson's Bay Company.[162] In addition to the twelve chief factors and six factors who accepted Wrigley's invitation, seven chief traders and four junior chief traders were included under special invitation when it was learned that they were in the city. They met for a week during which time 104 articles of the new rules and regulations were discussed, amended and passed. They covered every aspect of the fur trade: tariffs for supplies; regulations regarding officers, clerks and servants; district management; furs; inventories; accounts; requisitions; mails and packets; and councils.

The tariff for officers' and clerks' supplies, which was the source of much dissatisfaction, had been one of Wrigley's major concerns. The existing tariff was based on location and Wrigley argued that officers in the same department should be entitled to receive their supplies at the same rate regardless of their location. Consequently, the new tariff was based on the cost landed price at the individual department depot. Since duty on imported articles was uniform and freight charges only a small proportion of the cost landed, the average would vary only marginally for each department.

New rules for district management established the responsibilities of both the officer in charge and the post masters working under him. Posts were to be visited on a regular basis, unauthorized absences and competition between posts were forbidden and the practice of forwarding annual district and department reports was to be revived. In an attempt to preserve resources, out-of-season kills would henceforth be discouraged and officers agreed to assist in enforcing Dominion and provincial laws.

---

[162]J. Brown refers, in *The Beaver* (1921), to a council of fur trade officers held at Athabaska Landing in July 1898 but this is not substantiated by primary sources ("The 'Lords of the North' in Annual Conclave", p. 3).

Taken as a whole, the revised regulations reflected the new situation in which the company found itself and the more business-like approach taken by Wrigley towards the fur trade. Gone were rules pertaining to inland water routes and brigades, promoting moral and religious improvement and establishing prices for buffalo robes. Times and circumstances had changed and the newly drafted policies were concrete evidence of both the company's and Wrigley's commitment to meet the challenge. Commissioned officers were active participants, proposing amendments throughout the debate, many of which were adopted.[163]

If the commissioned officers had won concessions in the establishment of new regulations and a pension plan they were more than offset by Wrigley's announcement during the council that, in future, commissions would no longer be issued to clerks or servants who had entered the service after 1870.[164] The announcement was unanimously condemned among the officers. As a consequence, the traditional *esprit de corps* among company men was lost and, in ensuing years, the only interest most servants had was getting their salary.[165] In 1889, districts were enlarged due to the fact that no more commissions were being granted and there were fewer qualified men to run the business. This move, coupled with more frequent inspection tours, further helped to centralize control.

The decision to discontinue further commissions was the second last step in extinguishing the once proud tradition of commissioned officers in favour of a salaried system. In 1902 the apprenticeship system was discontinued and post managers became, to a large extent, men chosen from various fields of business or men who were raised and educated in the country, including "mixed bloods".[166]

Once the council concluded, Wrigley had one month to complete his general report on the company's trade. He had earlier requested that his visit to London to present the report be delayed until October to enable him to visit more districts and examine the Trading Year '86 accounts, which had not been finalized until July 1888.

It was a detailed report, listing actual gain or loss by outfit and assessing problems faced at every post in the four departments. The message was clear:

Wrigley's general discussion reiterated many of his concerns including competition, transportation costs, fur declines, native destitution, tariffs, operating costs and expenses. Detailed examination of post accounts revealed that profits were made

---

[163]Fifty-five amendments were proposed to the final 104 rules. Of these, 43 were recorded as having been adopted. Principal participants were Samuel Parsons, Lawrence Clarke, Roderick MacFarlane, Joseph Fortescue and Peter W. Bell who proposed or seconded 57 per cent of the amendments.

[164]It is curious that no mention was made of this announcement in any of the council minutes or in Armit's and Wrigley's correspondence both prior to and after the meeting.

[165]N.M.W.J. McKenzie, *The Men of the Hudson's Bay Company*, p. 46.

[166]H.A. Innis, *The Fur Trade in Canada*, p. 356.

TABLE 3 GAIN/LOSS BY DEPARTMENT, 1887-1888

Department	Trading Year 86	Trading Year 85	Net Gain	Net Loss
Northern	-191,794	-89,610	------	$281,404
Southern	-100,565	58,700	------	41,865
Montreal	- 51,210	-14,162	------	65,372
Western	- 22,343	4,912	------	17,431
			TOTAL LOSS	$406,072

(Source: Joseph Wrigley, *Report of the Commissioner to the Governor, Deputy Governor and Committee of the Hudson's Bay Company of the Trade of the Company*, n.p.)

primarily where fur collections were large even when trappers demanded high prices. Although improvements had been made, the present tariff system did not lend itself to a competitive market. Wrigley concluded that in a market where the future was always uncertain, the best policy was to buy freely when prices were low and exercise caution when they were high. Currently, company officers tended to do the opposite. Sales catalogues were helpful guides but they only indicated the realized price and gave no information concerning colour, condition, quality and size. The benefits of obtaining good information from American and European markets, he argued, far outweighed the cost involved and would only increase trading efficiency.

Competition could only increase and Wrigley believed that it could best be met by careful reduction of expenses coupled with an informed selection of goods, transportation improvements and the adoption of a definite trade policy based on the principle that expenses remained almost constant regardless of the size of the fur collection. While initial steps had been taken in this direction, further action would await the board's response to Wrigley's report.

Chapter 4

NEW STORES AND OLD PROBLEMS

When the board hired Joseph Wrigley it was eager to capitalize on new opportunities opening up in the Canadian west. The construction of the transcontinental railway and the growing numbers of immigrants who followed in its wake effectively ended the fur trade in settled areas but opened up new markets for retail and wholesale ventures.[167] As the fur trade declined in relative importance, the company planned to shift its focus to commercial enterprises such as mills and saleshops, headed by a man well versed in modern business principles.

Wrigley's initial arrival in Winnipeg was not auspicious. A severe storm had recently damaged the company's Fort Garry mill and stripped the roof from the old store, spoiling much of the stock. A new asphalt roof was quickly installed on the store but the grist mill had other problems. Like most of its rural counterparts, it had been built to attract settlers to the company's land holdings and as a market for grain offered in trade. Ideally, flour produced at the mill would be sold locally, shipped to northern posts or used for Indian Department contracts. By 1884, the company had mills at Edmonton, West Lynne [Manitoba], Fort Garry and Riding Mountain, and another stone mill was being reconstructed at Prince Albert. None of them, however, lived up to expectations. Their antiquated equipment could not compete with flour mills which had converted to the new roller processing method.[168] Unable to dispose of its stone ground flour which was unsuitable for government contracts, the company let the Fort Garry Mill stand idle, a steady drain on resources. The mill laboured under an additional handicap in that it was excluded from an arrangement with the city whereby some millers were exempt from taxes as compensation for their considerable outlay.[169]

----

[167]From 1881 to 1891 Winnipeg's population increased by 221% to 25,639 while Manitoba's population increased by 145% to 152,506 (Alan Artibise, *Winnipeg, An Illustrated History*, p. 200).

[168]This system, developed in Hungary, produced premium white flour from hard spring wheat by a system of gradual reduction using steel rollers. It was introduced to Manitoba in 1882 by the Ogilvie Milling Company and, by 1887, only stone mills distant from the railway were doing custom work; the rest had been forced to convert or close (*The Commercial*, 8 February 1887).

[169]When the Ogilvie brothers built in 1881, city council granted them a 20-year tax exemption (R. Rostecki, "The Growth of Winnipeg, 1870-1886", p. 74). After considerable lobbying, Wrigley succeeded in obtaining a similar exemption for the Fort Garry Mill in 1886 (HBCA, D.13/8, fo. 57d, Wrigley to Armit, 22 June 1886). Other exemptions are listed in HBCA, D.26/12, fos. 22-23, January 1886.

59

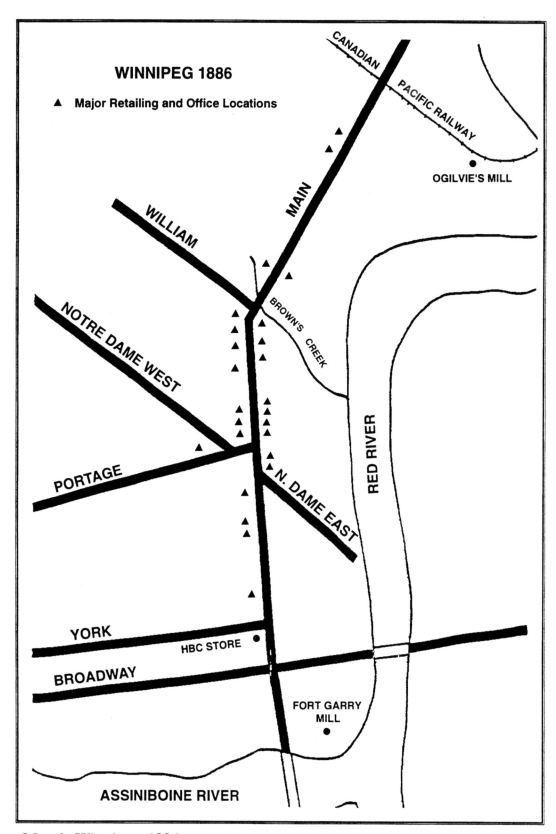

Map 2: Winnipeg, 1886

Wrigley acknowledged that too much money had already been sunk into the mills for the amount of business done and even more was required to buy premium grade flour from competitors to meet the company's needs. The choice was simple: convert or sell and within two weeks of taking office, Wrigley had drawn up a proposal for conversion of the Fort Garry Mill to rollers at a cost of $12,000. By November 1884 he had received the board's authorization to add a roller and purifier to the Prince Albert Mill, and the following January the *Free Press* reported that work had begun on the modernization of the Fort Garry Mill.[170]

The company's investment was not limited to the mill. Wrigley approached the CPR with a proposal to extend the railway from St. Boniface over the Broadway Bridge to the Fort Garry Mill, making it more competitive with Ogilvie's mill on the main rail line in Point Douglas. Rail access would save the company high cartage expenses and increased toll revenue would make it worthwhile for the Red River and Assiniboine Bridge Company, owners of the bridge, to strengthen it to the necessary levels. Wrigley consulted Land Commissioner Brydges, the founder of the Bridge Company[171] and, armed with Donald A. Smith's support for conversion of the mill to rollers, he set about getting estimates for the rail extension. The company offered land and right of way where needed and covered the cost of grading. The CPR agreed to supply rails and ties.[172] Wrigley assured the board that the investment was sound and, after some hesitation, it finally approved.

Once this was settled, Wrigley turned his attention to the Winnipeg Sales Shop. Located at York and Main, it had been constructed during the 1881 boom to attract a prosperous clientele. By 1884, there were 54 employees in the retail and wholesale business and eight clerks in the Northern Department Depot and General Office under the management of Factor William H. Adams.[173] When the boom collapsed, the company found itself sharing the plight of many other businesses faced with mounting debts and dwindling income. Distress sales become commonplace, placing even more pressure on still solvent merchants. In 1883 a special committee was organized by

---

[170]*Manitoba Free Press*, 20 January 1885.

[171]Brydges' overlapping roles as head of the Bridge Company and Land Commissioner for its major shareholder, the Hudson's Bay Company, appear blatantly irregular by today's conflict of interest regulations. The Bridge Company was founded in 1879 and built two toll bridges into the Company's land reserve: the Main Street Bridge, which channelled traffic past the new retail store, and the Broadway Bridge. Other directors included Donald A. Smith, James A. Grahame succeeded by Wrigley, and Sedley Blanchard, the company's solicitor (John Selwood, "Mr. Brydges' Bridges", pp. 14-21).

[172]HBCA, D.13/6, fo. 141, Wrigley to Armit, 4 March 1885.

[173]HBCA, D.38/4, "List of Commissioned Officers, Clerks and Postmasters H.B. Co. Western Department, 1885", p. 100.

retailers and wholesalers to arrange for the orderly disposal of bankrupt stocks, thus preventing slaughter prices which threatened the entire business community.[174]   In response to the board's demands to curb credit and collect outstanding debts, Wrigley argued that many large debts had been incurred by people he was anxious not to offend in the best interests of the company.   Among the worst offenders were Land Commissioner Brydges; the Manitoba Club, of which Brydges was President; and the CPR. Fur traders were also notorious for their high balances but the company could not risk restricting their credit for fear of losing their furs. Wrigley noted that "nearly everyone, even in the highest position, appears to be more or less embarrassed."[175] Many, trusting in the company's wealth and leniency, ignored their bills, considering the interest saved as a source of income. The company and other retailers trod a thin line. Inattention to overdue accounts guaranteed steady losses but stricter credit measures only alienated the more affluent clientele they sought to attract.

The store suffered from several disadvantages. It was located on the edge of an upper to middle class residential area away from the busiest part of the city, and therefore attracted only a small share of the working class trade. The new premises were too large for the current depressed market and were burdened by high maintenance costs, insurance rates and taxes.[176]   Many neighbouring offices and businesses such as the post office, custom office and the Canadian North West Land Company had relocated near the intersection of Portage Avenue and Main Street, drawing even more traffic away from the store. It was badly overstocked with luxury items purchased during the boom; carpets, lace and champagne languished on shelves, depreciating and collecting dust. Clearance sales were moderately successful but given the great number of them in a limited market such as Winnipeg, even suitable stock could not be disposed of in quantity.

The company's problems were compounded by the fact that other shopkeepers frequently allied with their creditors and bought back their own stock at reduced prices, making it even more difficult to compete. Increasing numbers of shops in the city and surrounding towns were steadily drawing customers away and the company's wholesale business had almost died out as a result of its own stringent credit regulations.

These concerns were addressed at the board's annual spring meeting in April 1885. Given the large amount of capital required for the fur and general trade and the increasing requests to extend operations into new settlements, the board decided to have Wrigley review the entire system. Specifically, it requested information on the amount

---

[174]R. Bellan, "The Development of Winnipeg as a Metropolitan Centre", p. 64.

[175]HBCA, D.13/7, fo. 49d, Wrigley to Armit, 17 November 1884. The Manitoba Club finally settled its debt in 1887 for 50 cents on the dollar. Wrigley considered this a satisfactory arrangement as the only alternative, bankruptcy, would deprive the company of substantial future cash sales.

[176]For another assessment of the stores's prospects, see HBCA, A.10/117, fos. 383-393, report from T.R. Smith to Armit, 8 July 1884.

of capital involved in each district, outstanding debts, stock on hand and profit/loss statements for the last three years. In addition, Wrigley was instructed to review the general system of accounts to assist the board in its plan to maintain a constant check over the company's operations.[177]

The situation was little better in the Western Department where the retail trade sector was relatively small, accounting for only one sixth of total sales. Most of the company's capital was invested in the Victoria wholesale trade where 90 days to settle accounts was commonplace. Any expansion in this area would automatically increase outstanding balances but if investment was cut back, retail trade would have to take up the slack. Otherwise the company would lose ground to the competition which could never be regained.

Wrigley cautioned against retail expansion in Victoria which was amply provided with stores. Instead, he recommended the establishment of a small store in Vancouver, anticipating its rise in economic dominance as a distribution centre when the railway was completed. The CPR had given the company two choice lots at the corner of Granville and Georgia Streets diagonally opposite the CPR's Hotel Vancouver. Until the area was more settled, however, Wrigley advised against building and authorized a temporary store on land leased from the CPR on Cordova Street.

A sharp increase in immigration to the west in the early 1880s was accompanied by growing numbers of independent traders. In response, company officers stepped up requests to open new retail outlets and upgrade old ones. Many trading posts were now dilapidated and located too far from reserves and settlements. Several post managers complained that business was being lost to competitors with better salesmanship and Wrigley recommended that the board hire more men with shopkeeping or warehouse experience. As an alternative, he proposed that newcomers serve a short apprenticeship at the Winnipeg store to learn the business.

He also sought the board's opinion on newspaper advertising, noting that the company was operating at a disadvantage in this area. Personally, he was distrustful of its merits. Just as he had found it distasteful to promote himself in his letter of application, he may have thought such advertising unsuitable for a business of the company's stature. His restraint was in direct contrast to the aggressive advertising campaigns mounted by Land Commissioner Charles Brydges. Even when repeatedly ordered to curtail advertising expenditures, Brydges continued to defend them, noting: "We spend a good deal less than others similarly situated and unless we let it be known that we have wares to sell we shall get few buyers. The Store here for a long time did not advertise at all but they are doing so now with considerable advantage."[178]

Another area that the company looked to for profit was government contracts to supply North West Mounted Police posts and Indian reserves. Its chief competitor was

---

[177]HBCA, A.1/152, fos. 241-242, 21 April 1885.

[178]H. Bowsfield (ed.), *The Letters of Charles John Brydges, 1883 - 1889*, p. 344, Brydges to Armit, 10 November 1888.

I.G. Baker & Sons, a Montana-based firm which had gradually expanded into the Canadian west and gained a virtual monopoly on cattle ranching, transportation, banking and mail service.

The company had been established at Fort Benton by the Baker brothers in 1866 when it was the only Indian trading post in the eastern two thirds of Montana.[179] With the arrival of competition the next year, the Bakers established a series of outposts which were successful in capturing most of the market in buffalo robes and furs. An influx of gold miners funded a steady cash trade which financed further expansion. In 1873, Charles, William and John Conrad became partners in the firm which now controlled the lion's share of the trade north from Fort Benton to Blackfoot territory. With their intimate knowledge of the area, it was only natural that they were consulted when the Canadian government decided to establish a North West Mounted Police post at Fort Walsh. I.G. Baker secured freighting and supply contracts for the police and government at Fort Walsh and Fort Macleod as well as for American army troops and supplied ranches and Indian reserves on both sides of the border. By the 1880s I.G. Baker was one of the largest and richest firms in the region, presenting formidable competition to the Hudson's Bay Company as its sphere of dominance widened.

Its major advantage over the Hudson's Bay Company was its Fort Benton location on the Missouri River.[180] One of Baker's subsidiaries, the Benton, Macleod and Calgary Stage Company, linked Fort Benton with Canadian towns and, until the arrival of the CPR, carried their mail to the east bearing American stamps.[181] As one of the founders of the Benton National Bank, I.G. Baker supplied cash for police payrolls and treaty payments that could not be handled from Winnipeg because of the limited transportation links with the east. As a result the region functioned as an economic unit with Canadian and American currency circulating freely on both sides of the border. As the business expanded, Isaac Baker returned to St. Louis to supervise his fleet of Missouri steamers leaving the Conrads to shape the firm's western policy.

One of the most lucrative aspects of the business was government contracts, and the winning of a major contract could spell the difference between success or failure for western businessmen. The awarding of large government contracts to American firms was unpopular among Canadian merchants, particularly those who supported the party in power. Despite numerous complaints and parliamentary investigations the Conrads managed to gain a monopoly due to their expertise, financial assets and geographic location. Political lobbying on both sides of the border was intense. Police and government officials were well known to and cultivated by the Conrads, and between 1875 and 1883 their company won all of the major freighting and supply contracts with

---

[179]HSM, MC49, box 1, folder 7, Notes on the Business of I.G. Baker & Co. at Fort Benton.

[180]Shipping costs on the Macleod-Fort Benton route were 6-8 cents/pound compared to 18 cents/pound by the Manitoba route (Paul Sharp, *Whoop-Up Country*, p. 218).

[181]Ibid., p. 188.

the police force averaging $100,000 per year. Lieutenant Governor Edgar Dewdney was responsible for many of I.G. Baker's Canadian contracts and, in return, he was granted handsome investments in Benton enterprises.[182] Even more lucrative were the contracts to supply beef to Indian reserves authorized by Treaties 4 and 7. Again, with its vast cattle ranches, I.G. Baker was the undisputed leader. Once contracts had been secured, the Conrads enlarged and protected them by a combination of public relations, bribery and monopolistic arrangements which neutralized the competition.

With the advance of railways into the American west, I.G. Baker lost the advantage it had held with its steamer fleet and the completion of the CPR in 1885 finally ended Fort Benton's economic dominance in the Canadian west. Seeing the handwriting on the wall, Charles Conrad and his regional rival, Thomas Charles [T.C.] Power, agreed in 1881 to divide up the government contracting business in return for one quarter of the other's contract profits.[183]

By equalizing access to supply routes, the CPR enabled the HBC to compete more effectively. By 1884 I.G. Baker appeared ready to retrench and offered to enter into negotiations with the HBC to sell its Canadian retail holdings in Fort Macleod, Fort Walsh and Calgary.[184] Realizing that, for once, the company had the upper hand, Wrigley informed Conrad that he would assess their stock on its own merit rather than paying a good price just to rid the company of the opposition. Adams' assistant, Thomas Hendry, was sent to inspect the Calgary stock which he described somewhat disdainfully as "American and inferior to the company's goods."[185] At the same time Conrad met with Wrigley to try and arrange a similar deal as that with T.C. Power whereby the two companies would divide up government contracts, each one taking a prescribed area. Although Wrigley awaited the board's instructions, he viewed such an arrangement with suspicion. The board declined either to deal or buy, agreeing with Wrigley that I.G. Baker would undoubtedly not remain long in Calgary. By June 1885, Wrigley reported with satisfaction that the company had obtained the greater part of the Indian contract, including the contract for flour, and for the remainder of the period to 1891, I.G. Baker's profits were derived mainly from its vast herds of cattle.

---

[182]In 1882 he was offered 40 shares in First National Bank of Fort Benton in return for his help in securing government deposits of between $100,000 and $200,000 (A. McCullough, "Papers Relating to the NWMP and Fort Walsh", pp. 22, 25, 27).

[183]James M. Francis, "Business Enterprise and the National Policy: the Role of T.C. Power & Brother and I.G. Baker & Company in the Political and Economic Development of the Southwestern Canadian Prairies and Northern Montana, 1870-1893", pp. 27-28. Although Power was Baker's major competitor, they had combined forces on several other occasions, notably as co-founders of the Benton National Bank and the Benton and St. Louis Cattle Company.

[184]HBCA, D.48, folder 8, I.G. Baker, St. Louis to HBC London, 21 August 1884.

[185]HBCA, D.14/8, fo. 564, Wrigley to Hardisty, Calgary, 16 February 1885.

A critical problem that the company faced in attempting to diversify its operations was to reconcile the conflicting demands of its various enterprises. This was aptly demonstrated by the bitter debate in Winnipeg over bridge tolls. By January 1886 the branch line over the Broadway Bridge to the Fort Garry mill was progressing despite the CPR's refusal to accept responsibility beyond the eastern edge of the bridge. Wrigley's headaches were just beginning. The next obstacle was setting the tolls to be paid by railway cars crossing the bridge to the mill. Disagreement developed immediately between Wrigley and Land Commissioner Brydges, president of the Bridge Company. Wrigley argued that the Hudson's Bay Company had built the line, funded jointly by the fur and land departments.[186] The Bridge Company stood to benefit from the upgrading of the bridge and now was trying to impose ruinous tolls. The increased cost would far outweigh any profit the company might realize and it would be forced, in turn, to raise the price of flour to cover expenses. He proposed instead that a regular sum be paid by the company to cover right of way and maintenance costs, but Brydges remained adamant that the Hudson's Bay Company should not receive preferential treatment.

TABLE 4 AMOUNTS AWARDED BY THE DEPARTMENT OF INDIAN AFFAIRS FOR SUPPLY CONTRACTS

YEAR ENDING	HBC	I.G. BAKER	T.C. POWER
1883	$ 32,618.10	$521,330.34	$ 497.29
1884	102,428.32	416,409.34	683.31
1885	229,812.60	265,453.79	12,478.48
1886	133,195.06	377,178.96[a]	0.00
1887	116,534.91	172,206.24[b]	5,710.27
1888	104,762.00	81,459.00[c]	304.09
1889	77,812.44	134,540.73[d]	0.00
1890	65,679.80	4,271.26	0.00
1891	101,371.46	112,607.86[e]	0.00

[a] Includes five orders for beef totalling $328,438.02.
[b] Includes four orders for beef totalling $156,582.77.
[c] Includes two orders for beef totalling $62,005.33.
[d] Includes two orders for bacon totalling $49,953.60 and three orders for beef totalling $48,638.36.
[e] Includes two orders for beef totalling $107,907.71.

(SOURCE: *Report of the Department of Indian Affairs*, Sessional Papers, 1883-1891.)

---

[186]Brydges authorized funding while Wrigley was involved in the North West Rebellion.

The matter was laid before the board which concluded that the two commissioners' figures were so much at variance that a decision could not be reached. Abdicating its responsibility to determine policy when presented with conflicting recommendations from its managers, the board returned the matter for further consideration.[187] As a potential winner no matter what was decided, the board no doubt felt it could afford to waffle. As a major shareholder in the bridge company, the company would benefit from higher tolls, and as an independent user its profits would be enhanced by a reduction.

After studying the mill's balance sheet for 1885-86 the board reluctantly concluded that if no agreement could be reached between the commissioners it would accept the subcommittee's compromise recommendation of $1.75 for full cars and fifty cents for empties, softening the blow for Wrigley with the promise of $10,000 for an elevator to hold grain which was currently being stored in the open.[188]

Wrigley never conceded that such tolls were justified. Over ensuing years his reports contained recurring requests for relief from high tolls which, he argued, placed the mill at a disadvantage in competing for contracts. Although he acknowledged that production costs were a major factor in the high price of flour, tolls also played a significant role. His position was supported in a report by James Anderson, comparing the Fort Garry Mill to Ogilvie's. In examining the question of shipping charges, Anderson concluded that for every $110.37 spent by Ogilvie the company had to pay $119.78, the difference arising from additional expenses in hauling cars over the bridge and shipping costs from the mill.[189] Brydges was equally unyielding. He professed an obligation to the bridge shareholders and in justice to their interests, could not consent to a reduction, suggesting, instead, that the company devote a portion of its annual dividend from the Bridge Company to meet the charges.[190]

Wrigley compensated for his failure to obtain toll concessions by victories in other areas of the trade. Claiming total profits of £83,667 in fur and general trade[191]

---

[187]HBCA, D.19/13, n.f., Extract from Board Minutes, 16 February 1886 enclosed in a letter from Armit to Wrigley, 18 February 1886.

[188]Wrigley's original proposal was $1.00 for a full car and fifty cents for an empty one. Brydges countered with $2.00 and $1.00.

[189]HBCA, D.13/8, fo. 289d, memo from Anderson to Wrigley, September 1887. When presented with the facts the CPR argued that the extra expense was to cover the cost of the siding and extra shunting and declined to reduce the surcharge.

[190]HBCA, D.48, folder 37, Brydges to Armit, 24 March 1887.

[191]HBC, *Report*, 29 June 1886, p. 5. A major flaw in the company's accounting system was the combination of general and fur trade accounts, making it virtually

(continued...)

for Trading Year '84, and in hopes that Manitoba's economy had finally bottomed out, the board loosened its purse strings. A new brick store was authorized at Rat Portage [Kenora] to replace one destroyed by fire. The ailing Portage la Prairie shop was relocated to a more central location and separate premises were purchased in Winnipeg to house the Winnipeg store's liquor shop. A new store was constructed at Fort Macleod to serve a large ranching community and nearby Indian reserves as well to improve the company's chances of securing local contracts. Wrigley also considered extending trade in southern Manitoba where the best quality of wheat was being produced by a rapidly expanding "good class of settlers."[192] A foothold had been gained at Morden and Manitou and new sales shops were proposed for La Rivière, a divisional point on the CPR, and Deloraine, the terminus of the Southwestern Railway.[193] In September 1886 the company and the CPR announced that they would jointly put their new town site at Fort William [Thunder Bay] on the market and shortly after, new stores were opened at Battle River, Alberta and Shoal Lake and Boissevain in Manitoba.[194]

Despite the care taken in selecting men to take charge of the small sales shops, it was acknowledged that they were quite unlike officers of former times who had a long standing loyalty to the company. Times had changed and with the expanding cash trade in settled areas, managers now handled considerable sums of money. A theft at the Portage la Prairie sales shop in October 1887 changed the way in which stores would be managed thereafter. Although there was no suspicion of embezzlement in this particular case, Wrigley proposed that it would be wise in future to require security from company servants involved in cash trade. The need for bonded clerks became even more apparent when Mr. Macrae, the company's clerk at West Lynne, fled to the United States with $500 of the company's money followed shortly thereafter by a Fort Garry Mill employee. Managers were subsequently instructed to ensure that a guard slept on the ground floor

---

[191](...continued)
impossible to determine their individual status. Complaints were raised annually by shareholders but to no avail, the board insisting that the accounts were amalgamated in accordance with the terms of the Deed Poll of 1871 whereby the commissioned officers were entitled to share equally in the profits of both divisions. Also, the board considered it unwise to do anything that would give the competition further knowledge of the company's retail business (HBC, *Proceedings*, 26 June 1883, pp. 15-17).

[192]HBCA, D.13/8, fo.191d, Wrigley to Armit, 4 April 1887.

[193]Several of these sales shops, such as the one at Manitou, started out in rented premises and, when the business had proven itself, a more permanent arrangement was made through the purchase of land or buildings.

[194]*The Commercial*, 30 November 1886, 18 January 1887 and 27 June 1887. For a case study of the transformation of company fur trade posts into general stores and the creation of a network of small department stores, see Henry C. Klassen, "The Hudson's Bay Company in Southwestern Alberta, 1874-1905".

and windows and doors were secured. Where possible, an account was to be opened at the local bank. Otherwise, sums larger than $100 were to be forwarded to the Department Office at the first opportunity.[195]

Wrigley's major report, presented to the board in November 1888, dealt at length with the company's retail operations as well as its fur and wholesale trade. In speaking of sales shops in general, Wrigley noted that there were now relatively few places where mercantile business was not combined with fur trading. In remote areas, the company had the competitive advantage of its capital reserves and prestige. But in cities and small towns where its sales shops housed dry goods, groceries and other departments, it was forced to compete with shopkeepers who specialized in only one area to which they could devote all their energy and capital, providing a much wider selection of goods. The company attempted to address this problem by keeping small quantities of a variety of items on hand and relying on telegraph, mail and railway to replenish depleted stocks. Slow-moving items were no longer allowed to sit and depreciate as they had in the past. Now they were sold off at clearance prices or transferred to another location and every effort was made to turn over capital as quickly as possible.

In the 1880s, most of the company's sales shops were located in areas where the population was likely to remain constant for the foreseeable future. Many suffered from unsuitable locations and business was lost even where a town's trading volume was large. Profits in smaller shops were often eaten up by fixed expenses, raising the question whether more money could be made in larger cities and more established towns as opposed to places where prospects were uncertain.

The ease with which credit could be secured from competitors presented another major problem. In agricultural areas in which most of the sales shops were located, it was difficult to secure cash payments until after the harvest. Wrigley emphasized, however, that great care was being taken in extending credit as current laws rendered the collection of debts by legal process very difficult. There were no bankruptcy laws in the Dominion and allowances of property exempt from seizure in Manitoba and the North West Territories were generous. The sentiment still existed that the company was rich and if it incurred debt no one in particular suffered. Consequently, the company was often forced to rely on the honesty of its customers for payment.

Another concern was that it was no longer sufficient for a commissioned officer in charge of a department to be skilled in the art of fur trading. He must also be well acquainted with the mercantile business, a good accountant and a skilled buyer in almost every market. Officers were at a disadvantage in not having expertise in dry goods and groceries where they were called upon to make extensive purchases. Few, in Wrigley's estimation, were capable of learning the principles of modern trade. In many cases, sales shop expenses were driven up by officers maintaining a large staff more typical of a fur

---

[195]HBCA, D.14/11, fo.112., Circular, n.d., Precautions to be adopted in all Sales Shops and at Posts in which cash is received.

trade post and by their unwillingness to recognize that circumstances had changed.[196] Their reluctance to acknowledge that a retail trader must be a servant of the public rather than a master of the trade did little to attract customers and was reflected in the lack of order and arrangement in their shops.[197]   Company shopkeepers who were not commissioned officers received a salary which remained independent of the margin of profit or loss. As an incentive to them, Wrigley suggested that the board offer them a share of the profits along with a small guaranteed minimum salary.

The Western Department found itself at a distinct disadvantage. Neglect of local demands had been endemic with indents often repeated from one year to the next with no consideration of changes in local conditions. It was increasingly obvious that goods which were popular in English markets were not necessarily suitable for the colonial trade. Although the department heads were competent, they were prevented by cost from visiting Canadian and American suppliers, and the company suffered as a result. Because the company required such large amounts of goods and paid cash promptly for all its purchases, Wrigley felt it should be able to obtain supplies on most favourable terms. At present, it could not do so since different buyers were making purchases in a variety of places and in smaller quantities rather than buying in bulk from a few sources.

To improve the situation, Wrigley recommended that all groceries should be purchased by officers in charge of the Winnipeg, Victoria and Montreal Depots. As for dry goods, one trustworthy and competent buyer should be appointed who knew the market thoroughly, was acquainted with the company's requirements, and had spent sufficient time in the three depots to gain a thorough knowledge of their needs. Thomas Hendry, Adams' assistant at the Winnipeg Sales Shop, was recommended as a likely candidate who could visit England several times a year to make recommendations regarding the selection of goods. A similar system had been adopted for the Northern Department Depot and recent district officers' reports testified to the improved selection of depot goods.

Wrigley also advised that the company make every effort to buy directly from manufacturers and avoid middlemen. This, he argued, should be feasible if cash was paid promptly. In districts where year-round communication existed, Wrigley proposed that annual English indents be abolished in favour of orders from the nearest depot which carried the same stock making that depot responsible for meeting the districts' demands. This would reduce the stock on hand at the posts and ensure a better assortment. The resultant savings would outweigh the small increase in capital investment at the depots.

---

[196]Douglas MacKay summed up the disdain many officers held for sales shops, describing them as "curiously transplanting to the prairie the dingy gentility of the drapery establishment of English provincial towns" (*The Honourable Company*, p. 304).

[197]For an analysis of the role of window displays in the late nineteenth century, see Keith Walden, "Speaking Modern: Language, Culture, and Hegemony in Grocery Window Displays, 1887-1920".

Again, cheaper rates could be obtained by buying in carload lots, although in some cases the company would lose the advantage of through rates as goods would no longer go straight through to the post.

Sales shop managers were anxious to obtain cheap goods and flashy novelties offered by their competitors but because the company traded largely on its prestige, great care was needed in yielding to their pressure. The best compromise, Wrigley concluded, was to stock cheaper goods in addition to, rather than instead of, the high quality of stock in which the company traditionally dealt. The future, Wrigley promised, would see considerable improvements, with increased emphasis being placed on goods best suited to the local market and giving the highest profit.[198]

In assessing individual sales shops (see Table 5), Wrigley touched first on Victoria whose profits had plummeted from $4,431 the previous year to $54.[199] Prior to Wrigley's arrival, business in both the fur and mercantile trade had been conducted in an unsatisfactory manner but the new assistant commissioner, T.R. Smith, was making considerable changes. The major portion of the trade was the wholesale supplying of shopkeepers and traders throughout the province based on credit, with cash sales accounting for only 10 per cent of the business. Many traders were becoming reckless, secure in the knowledge that if they failed, the loss would fall on the company as their creditor.

Retail trade had been allowed to pass into the hands of competitors and would now be difficult and expensive to regain. Neither the building nor the location in Victoria was suitable for a retail outlet and both time and new premises on a main thoroughfare would be required before much hold could be re-established. The completion of the railway had stimulated population growth but the entire district was overrun with competition as many of the settlers were small shopkeepers. Unless further large mineral deposits were found, Wrigley feared that British Columbia would be unable to support further population growth as the lumbering and fishing industries could not absorb many more workers.

In the Western Department competing retail shops were often attached to canneries and sawmills with relatively large concentrations of labour. As a result there was strong pressure from the officers for the company to enter into similar operations. Although this would place added demands on operating capital and force the company to compete with already established businesses, Wrigley could see no reason why, with care and as population increased, a satisfactory return on investment could not be obtained. The main question was whether the wholesale business should continue to monopolize the capital allotted to the department or whether a portion of it could be used more profitably in the retail business.

---

[198]Wrigley, *Report*, pp. 169-176.

[199]For a detailed description of the company's operations at Victoria, see *The Commercial*, 27 August 1888.

TABLE 5 NET TRADING PROFIT / LOSS,
HUDSON'S BAY COMPANY SALES SHOPS

LOCATION	TRADING YEAR 85	TRADING YEAR 86
Calgary	$ 6,750	$ 6,547
Fort Macleod	N/A	- 2,736
Keewatin	N/A	- 347
Manitou	1,587	- 567
Morden	- 844	- 2,027
Portage la Prairie	- 3,779	4,731
Rat Portage	664	- 3,850
Sudbury	N/A	- 497
Vancouver	N/A	N/A
Victoria	4,431	54
West Lynne	-10,953	- 441
Winnipeg	-16,728	-21,182

(SOURCE: Joseph Wrigley, *Report*, pp. 11, 14-15, 31, 54-60, 66, 74, 121, 138)

The Vancouver trade, on the other hand, was prospering, recording sales of $48,044 as opposed to $16,466 for the same period the previous year. Since it had been selected as the terminus of the CPR Wrigley concluded that it would likely become the mercantile capital of the province. Profits from the Calgary store remained steady at around $6,650 with an average turnover of three times a year. Its ideal location on the telegraph and rail line meant that supplies could be ordered frequently in small amounts which tied up less capital.[200]

In comparison, the Saskatchewan District recorded a loss of $13,678. The area had experienced several years of poor harvests but its problems went much deeper. As an area of small scattered settlements, its population was sufficient to eliminate furbearers but insufficient to enable the company to sustain a profitable commercial business. The inevitable outcome was confirmed by individual accounts for Prince Albert, Battleford, Fort Pitt, Fort Qu'Appelle and Fort Ellice which fell far short of expectations.

The Red River District had suffered an even worse fate with profits plummeting from $30,123 to a loss of $10,337 in Trading Year '86. In this area of primarily mercantile business, all but one post suffered from active competition. Factor W.H. Adams oversaw the entire district, including the Winnipeg Sales Shop and Northern Department Depot, and handled all the buying for the Northern Department. It was agreed that it was far too much responsibility for one man and new arrangements were being considered. As a temporary measure, purely fur trade posts along Lake Winnipeg

---

[200]Wrigley, *Report*, p. 31.

were amalgamated into a sub-district. The remainder of the district would be confined to general business which, because of the persisting depression, was not expected to increase until the population grew.

Curiously, the report made little mention of Indian and North West Mounted Police contracts. Wrigley noted in passing that, although contract profits were declining yearly, they still had a beneficial effect on district accounts through freight and handling charges.

After forwarding copies of his report to Secretary Armit, Wrigley left for New York where he boarded a ship for London. His meetings with the governor and committee in October 1888 coincided with the election of Donald A. Smith to the position of Deputy-Governor, succeeding Sir John Rose who had died unexpectedly the previous August. Within three months Governor Eden Colvile resigned, pleading ill health, and Smith became governor, the first in the company's history to have been actively involved in the Canadian trade. He had both the knowledge and power to govern unchallenged. With a new governor, and with Wrigley's report in hand giving the company its first accurate assessment of its overseas operations, the board embarked on a vigorous program of retrenchment.

Chapter 5

"SHOOTING THE MESSENGER"

The board responded to Wrigley's report just prior to the annual General Court in December 1888. He had forewarned the commissioned officers that board members and shareholders were convinced that expenses could be cut considerably without harm to the fur trade and the board's directives confirmed his fears.

To reduce the large number of inferior furs taken, the board ordered tickets attached to every pelt indicating its source. Records kept in London, combined with the realized price from each sale, would then serve as the basis on which post management would be judged.[201] Fur tariffs would now be set by district and they would determine trading limits rather than the average price which had encouraged trading for poor quality furs in the past.

Every effort was to be made to protect the barter system. With this in mind, greater latitude in trading furs was extended to officers in the Athabaska, Peace and English River districts as well as the Southern Department to prevent furs from being taken out and sold for cash in urban markets. Monthly reports of fur collections were now required from each district and a more efficient packing system was adopted whereby each species would be sorted into separate bales. In districts plagued by competition, advances would only be made to loyal friends of the company and credit would no longer be extended to those purchasing goods to trade inland.

In future, employment needs would be strictly defined and temporary assistants would be employed only as needed, the guiding principle being that every officer and servant should be fully employed at all times. To economize further, officers were now expected to spend more time trading or keeping accounts and if cuts in imports and staff failed to improve the balance sheet, posts would face closure.

After studying Wrigley's report on the Fort Garry mill, detailing ongoing competition from Ogilvie and unavoidable maintenance expenses and bridge tolls, the board gladly agreed to consider disposing of all of the company's mills.

In the area of retail trade, the board established limits on retail stock on hand and outstanding balances. The most unprofitable departments in the Winnipeg sales shop were discontinued, staff reduced and the implications of closing one floor of the store considered. Board members approved Wrigley's recommendation of Thomas Hendry, Factor Adams' assistant, as dry goods buyer; but to reduce expenses incurred by lengthy visits to England twice a year, they sent Godfrey Parker, superintendent of the company's London packing department, to visit Winnipeg and Victoria to determine the requirements of the respective depots. A shopkeeper from England was to be hired to

---

[201]This system, which was a reworking of the one proposed by Wrigley in 1887, was devised by and credited to Edward Harris, the board member who had vetoed the initial proposal.

relieve Adams of some of his duties. In return, Adams was appointed sales shop inspector and ordered to make an immediate inspection tour.

TABLE 6 NET TRADING LOSS - HUDSON'S BAY COMPANY MILLS

LOCATION	TRADING YEAR 85	TRADING YEAR 86
Edmonton	$2,095.	$ N/A
Fort Garry	1,911.	15,499.
Prince Albert	3,133.	2,878.
Riding Mountain	3,613.	1,602.
West Lynne	3,273.	2,502.

(SOURCE: Joseph Wrigley, *Report*, pp. 12-13)

Before accepting the inspectorship Adams prepared a report on the Winnipeg Sales Shop.[202] He felt that the sales shop itself was an attraction and if its general appearance was altered business would suffer. At present a considerable portion of the store was used by the depot and part of one floor was already closed off. A reduction of salaries totalling $3500 was being effected but further staff cuts would injure trade as there were often more customers in the store than could be served. He cautioned that, to remain competitive, the store must not appear scantily stocked. In future, smaller and more frequent indents would be made but any major changes would await Parker's arrival.

In response to Wrigley's concerns regarding sales shop security, the board instructed him to forward a list of shopkeepers employed in each department. The board agreed to assume the cost of bonding those already employed but newcomers would be hired on the condition that they were responsible for the guarantee premium.

Expansion of fur and retail trade in the Western Department was frozen until unprofitable posts could be closed. The board concluded that attempting to regain the company's former hold on retail trade would involve considerable outlay which prospects did not warrant and that the best route to follow was the general rule of cost reduction wherever possible.

Wrigley questioned the board's demand for immediate changes in management, preferring to delay such decisions until inspection reports could be examined. He defended capital expenditures in inland districts as barely exceeding what was necessary for the trade. Only withdrawal would bring any noticeable reductions and this Wrigley did not recommend, for once the company's hold was relaxed, it was not easily regained.

---

[202]HBCA, D.13/8, fos. 500d-501d, Wrigley to Armit, 7 January 1889.

But the board was losing patience. In response to Wrigley's request for a raise, no doubt based on his perception of a job well done, Governor Colvile was curt.

> As anticipated your application didn't commend itself to members especially at this time. I think you well to exercise patience in this matter and in the meanwhile to carry out loyally and energetically the instructions conveyed in the letter you took out with you and I think the sooner you set to work at this the better.[203]

The board also moved swiftly to stamp out opposition from a small group of shareholders, led by Robert A. McLean, who supported the adoption of policies that would capitalize on the company's land interests where they still believed its future lay, rather than on the fur trade whose prospects they considered dim. A circular to this effect demanded a more vigorous land policy, the election of younger men with commercial experience to the board and separate, more comprehensive accounts in the fur trade and land departments, putting an end to the combination of general and fur trade accounts which made it virtually impossible to determine their individual worth. Ignoring shareholders' annual complaints, the board had always insisted that the company was bound by the terms of the 1871 Deed Poll whereby commissioned officers were entitled to share equally in the profits of both divisions.

The board's response to McLean's group was predictable. A more detailed system of accounting could do harm, it argued, by providing more information to the competition. Led by Deputy-Governor Donald A. Smith, it supported the election of Russell Stephenson to the board over McLean at the December 1888 General Court, despite complaints that Stephenson had been a shareholder for only one month.[204] Stephenson was elected and McLean's resolution to divide shares into two classes, fur trade and land, was soundly defeated at a special General Court held in July 1889, presided over by Governor Smith.

In early 1889, the newly elected governor Smith made clear his intention to centralize control in his directives to Wrigley regarding personnel changes, traditionally the sole prerogative of the trade commissioner. Land Commissioner Charles Brydges, who had a long history of conflict with Smith, soon found his job in jeopardy.[205] At the December General Court, the board had concluded that the salary of the land commissioner was out of proportion to the amount of business transacted and Smith was authorized to find a temporary replacement. Unknown to Brydges, the position was

---

[203]HBCA, A.7/5, fo. 110, Colvile to Wrigley, 13 December 1888.

[204]For a fuller discussion of McLean's opposition, see Sealey, "History of the HBC, 1870-1900", pp. 59-63.

[205]For a discussion of the relationship between Donald A. Smith and Charles Brydges, see Shirlee A. Smith, "'A Desire to Worry Me Out', Donald Smith's Harassment of Charles Brydges, 1879-1889".

offered in turn to Chief Factor Alex Munro of Victoria and to Mr. Browning, a successful Vancouver real estate dealer, both of whom declined. During these negotiations, Brydges died unexpectedly and Wrigley assumed temporary control of the land department until Factor James H. Lawson of the Victoria office was appointed to the lesser position of land agent.

As the new buying season approached, the board urged further cost cuts. A four per cent profit on Indian and police contracts was considered inadequate since this did not take into account store or department expenses, and it instructed Wrigley to submit tenders only if an adequate profit was assured. Newspaper advertising expenses in both the land and fur trade departments were considered excessive and Wrigley was cautioned that a more moderate amount should suffice.

Wrigley's complaints that the company was losing furs under the current tariff provoked criticism for his apparent disregard for previous directives. His authority was further weakened by orders that all district reports be prepared in triplicate, the third copy to be sent to the Canadian subcommittee, a system similar to that already adopted in the Western Department. The absence of relevant reports at year end, not uncommon given the vast distances involved, nevertheless prompted the board's observation that "business is not conducted with that careful supervision which is absolutely necessary to ensure its success."[206]

Wrigley's communications with the commissioned officers in turn became more abrupt as he embarked on a series of major personnel changes. Chief Trader Alex Matheson was ordered to reduce Indian debts at Rat Portage or "I shall be obliged to take steps which I should much regret."[207] T.R. Smith of Victoria was ordered to pension off employees, give up unprofitable parts of the trade, produce missing balance sheets and run monthly rather than yearly audits on cash accounts while he continued to insist that he could make the business pay if only he was given free scope.

To maintain closer control over inventories, the board instructed Wrigley to consider the individual merits of each indent before he approved it. However, as he reminded its members, he had no way of knowing how much capital had already been invested in each district and he had practically no control over purchases made in the Montreal and Western Departments which indented directly on London. In the past, since each successive outfit merely listed an inventory of assets plus the shipments made to England, it was impossible to prepare orderly statements of profit and loss or to make detailed comparisons of one year's business with another. Consequently, the cost of the fur trade payroll was unknown, as were the amounts of money drawn on London, the amount of goods forwarded and to what uses the money was applied.

His arguments, coupled with the shareholders' demands for a better accounting system, finally bore fruit. A memo from the company's auditor was forwarded to Wrigley in April 1889, outlining recommendations to modernize the accounting system

---

[206]HBCA, D.19/16, fo. 8, Armit to Wrigley, 15 January 1889.

[207]HBCA, D.14/12, fo. 323, Wrigley to Matheson, 2 February 1889.

by changing it from single entry to double entry. The new system would finally place control of indents in the hands of the commissioner, thus reducing the initiative of officers to secure supplies from alternative sources.[208]

The goal of the proposed accounting reforms, which were intended to enhance rather than replace the current system, was to record assets and liabilities on current accounts, the amount of capital employed and the measure of business transacted on each post's balance sheet as well as to create a proper payroll for all company servants and clerks. Success would depend on whether proper ledgers could be introduced at the post level and whether officers could prepare more complex returns. Wrigley assured the board that the new system would be used for Trading Year '88 but he cautioned that the lack of accounting skills among fur traders in general had to be taken into account. Chief Factor Samuel Parsons, head of the Montreal Department, and Junior Chief Trader Edmund K. Beeston, the company's Winnipeg accountant, expressed similar concerns but the board insisted that every effort be made to have the new trading accounts prepared at every post where possible.

The officers' doubts were well founded. Many excellent traders and servants could not fill out the simplest records and instructing them by mail rarely worked. Where doubt existed, lack of communication made it almost impossible to verify and adjust the figures.

By May 1889 the inspection report of the Winnipeg Sales Shop was completed. It contained few surprises. The main problem was the large volume of surplus stock on which clearance sales had little effect. The board accepted Godfrey Parker's and Factor Adams' recommendations that laces, silks and grenadine be shipped to Toronto and Montreal to be sold in lots by tender. The remainder would be moved to a temporary location in the city centre and sold off after the harvest when best prices could be obtained. Although the loss would be great, $20,000 being projected, almost all could be disposed of except boots and shoes which would be auctioned off in Montreal. In this manner, the goods would be removed from inventory and their loss spread out over the subsequent three outfits.

Wrigley was instructed to give the Winnipeg sales shop his daily personal attention and to exercise control over its management as well as over that of the other main sales shops. Consequently, he directed each sales shop to submit monthly statements outlining capital expenditures, stock on hand and outstanding balances.

Despite agreement on what had to be done it was difficult to translate ideas into action as many of the commissioned officers continued to find it difficult to adapt to a new way of doing business. Although the Saskatchewan District was the worst offender, it was symptomatic of the entire system of operations. Lawrence Clarke, whose future was in jeopardy, was told repeatedly to reduce stock on hand in his district sales shops. Debts and Indian gratuities were too high as were his prices, all of which were to be reduced at once. Stock was often unsuited to the trade and more attention was needed to the art of window dressing. Although Wrigley defended his friend, insisting he was

---

[208]Ibid., p. 110.

still the best person to put the district into a proper state, he agreed to bow to the board's wishes if it ordered Clarke removed.[209]

Store managers in rural areas were asked to reassess the value of advertising and discouraged from purchasing from independent traders no matter how attractive their goods. They were instructed, instead, to buy from the depot which had the advantage in buying in bulk and could be visited in May and December when travellers' samples were shown.[210]

To further complicate matters, W.H. Adams had returned to England for three months of rest on the advice of his doctor and asked to be relieved of his inspectorship. The staff shortage was alleviated somewhat by the appointment of Godfrey Parker as head of the depot and chief buyer for both the depot and the Sales Shop under orders from the trade commissioner. Adams' assistant, Thomas Hendry, was transferred to the Western Department as an assistant to T.R. Smith.[211] While his buying was considered satisfactory for the depot, his taste did not suit the sales shop's urban clientele.

Although the Western Department appeared to be the only one which adopted the new accounting procedures with any success, due to the talents of its accountant, A.J. Simpson, this progress was overshadowed by chronic problems. In his annual pessimistic report on that department, Wrigley noted that the nature of the trade along the Northwest Coast had changed dramatically during the last few years with the establishment of independent canneries and sawmills which siphoned off much of the trade and provided wage employment for the native population. Junior Chief Trader Robert H. Hall, a dynamic force in the area, was discouraged by the closing of many inland posts. The company's decision to withdraw when faced by even the slightest competition had resulted in a general lowering of its image, and Wrigley again urged that a steamer on the Skeena River would do much to reduce freight rates and render the company independent of general freighters.

The board held fast to its original decision. It regretted Wrigley's decision to hire someone from outside the company to do an unauthorized navigational assessment of the Skeena River. The resultant report would place information in the hands of other interested parties and if a steamer could reduce transportation costs, others would follow the company's lead and gain equal advantage. Wrigley's disappointment and frustration were evident in his response: "I will not, however, now venture to submit that the views of the board are not the best for the interests of the company; at any rate they shall be loyally carried out."[212]

---

[209]In the end, Wrigley was spared having to ask for Clarke's resignation as he died suddenly in October 1890.

[210]HBCA, D.14/12, fos. 828-829d, Wrigley to E. Gigot, Fort Macleod, 30 July 1889 and D.14/13, fo. 168, Wrigley to G.S. Davidson, Prince Albert, 21 November 1890.

[211]HBCA, D.13/9, fo. 62, Wrigley to Armit, 30 December 1889.

[212]HBCA, D.13/9, fo. 65, Wrigley to Armit, 9 January 1890.

In other areas, expansion was needed. Wrigley recommended new stores for Sudbury and Calgary where the company's wooden buildings appeared shabby beside new stone structures and trade was being lost for lack of suitable premises. The arrival of the railway in Edmonton promised increased business and Wrigley cautioned Junior Chief Trader Harrison Young to exercise caution in making advances to freighters. The prospect of a two storey stone building to replace the Edmonton townsite shop, once considered the finest store west of Winnipeg, prompted Wrigley to request Young to devise a scheme whereby customers would be prevented from obtaining credit at both the townsite and fort locations.

The Vancouver area was also booming. There had been substantial construction in the west end of the city and trade appeared to be recovering from the depression. T.R. Smith had often complained that many fine buildings were going up nearby while the company's land remained vacant. It was agreed that the company needed a good store, well stocked and smartly fitted. Half measures would not suffice and Wrigley urged the company to demonstrate its faith in the city's prospects by showing a reasonable disregard for cost. A branch store had been opened in rented premises in the Crewe Block on Granville Street housing millinery, menswear, carpet and dressmaking departments. Nothing permanent was done, however, until the spring of 1892 when the three storey "New Store" was constructed on Granville, immediately opposite the Donald A. Smith block, boasting a central elevator similar to one seen in Seattle and travelling overhead cash railways.[213] Both T.R. Smith and Charles Robson, manager of the store, agreed that it would be wise to limit trade to cash as much as possible, conducting the business along the lines of the London Co-operative Stores.

At the same time that Wrigley was recommending expansion in Calgary, Charles Conrad revived the offer of sale of I.G. Baker & Sons' Canadian retail operations. The new offer included I.G. Baker's businesses at Fort Macleod, Lethbridge and Calgary which were no longer considered profitable because they had kept larger stock, taken more risks, and held mortgages and other securities in which the company did not deal. If the company did not buy these facilities, he warned, a joint stock company would be formed which could offer strong competition for contracts. Governor Smith again declined to buy.[214] Undaunted, Conrad put forth a second proposal asking $200,000 for Baker's stock and real estate in return for the right to retain its cattle business.[215]

Upon consideration of a report on I.G. Baker's operations the HBC offered $44,000 for its land and buildings. Saleable goods would be purchased at a reduction of 20 per cent on cost landed and the remainder at a mutually agreed price. Customer credit was to be turned over to the company as part of the purchase price but all outstanding balances were to be collected by I.G. Baker & Sons on the understanding that they not take legal action against any of these customers for a specified time without the

---

[213]H.T. Lockyer, "The Rise of H.B.C. Vancouver Retail Establishment", pp. 20-21.

[214]HBCA, D.13/9, fos. 84-85, memo for the Governor, n.d.

[215]HBCA, D.19/17, fo. 141, Conrad to Smith, 1 May 1890.

company's sanction. Conrad also agreed to trade at company stores and withdraw from all but beef contracts.[216] The deal was successfully concluded with Wrigley negotiating a final reduction of 25 per cent on cost landed for saleable goods with the remainder taken at valuation.

On the whole, Wrigley felt the deal was advantageous although its ultimate success would depend on the general prosperity of the country and the management of the business. The papers were no sooner signed when Conrad sought to buy back property in Calgary and Lethbridge at 10 per cent above purchase price, in order to open butcher shops. Wrigley agreed, noting that neighbouring butcher shops would be advantageous to the company in attracting customers. The final transfer was set for the end of March 1891 but when he heard that Conrad was selling stock at cost, Wrigley ordered the transfer to proceed immediately. By 9 March, the Calgary stock and fixtures had been taken over for $25,523 and valuations at Fort Macleod were complete.[217] A week later Wrigley was able to report that cash sales amounting to $805 and credit sales of $838 had been completed in what was considered the dullest season of the year. At this rate, he hoped that by the end of March enough would have been taken in to cover the cost of the first instalment.

If Wrigley had any hopes that the new year would signal a fresh start, they were soon dashed by a letter from board secretary Armit regarding officers' and servants' overdrawn accounts. The state of these accounts had been an ongoing concern. In March 1886 a resolution had been passed directing Wrigley to collect arrears in the Northern Department where overdrafts were particularly serious.[218] It had been hoped that the new rules and regulations, passed in 1888, would bring about an improvement but now the board observed that instructions had not been carried out and placed the onus solely on Wrigley. Armit's letter did not reach Wrigley before he left on his annual trip to Montreal. Instead, he was handed a copy by Governor Smith upon arrival and requested to draft a reply before returning to Winnipeg.

Wrigley explained that he had not understood that he was personally responsible for collecting officers' overdrafts. Believing these accounts were private matters between the officer and the board, he considered his duty fulfilled by advising the men as instructed. Acknowledging the seriousness of the matter, he proposed sending monthly statements to district officers outlining their advances and asking them to report periodically on their status. Currently, advances were reported only at the close of each outfit and the adoption of this plan would enable Wrigley to maintain tighter control. Wrigley expressed concern at the strong tone of Armit's letter, stating that he knew of no single instance where he had failed to carry out instructions and would not knowingly fail to do so.

---

[216]Ibid., fo. 184, Armit to Wrigley, 9 December 1890.

[217]Ibid., fo. 291, Wrigley to Armit, 9 March 1891.

[218]HBCA, A.1/153, fos. 68-69.

The board continued to snipe, citing debts wrongly written off and unauthorized money spent on new buildings. Wrigley scrambled to defend himself. He admitted that the board's decision to veto the Skeena steamer had escaped his memory, but he pointed out that Governor Smith had supported Junior Chief Trader Hall's original recommendations. Competition already existed at Hazelton, which was the key to New Caledonia, and cheap transportation was the only means of checking it. Wrigley held fast however, against criticism of his lack of enforcement of the new rules and regulations which set limits on the amount officers were entitled to take in cash advances. He reminded the board that when he assumed his position there were practically no regulations and discipline was decidedly lax. Being new to the company, he chose to wait several years before taking active steps. The new rules had received the board's sanction but they had not been fully understood by the officers and there had been difficulty in convincing them that they must be followed.

His arguments appeared to have some effect and the board relented with regard to the Skeena steamer. In a complete turnaround, board members expressed pleasure at Hall's persistence in advocating a policy advantageous to his district even though they knew he felt that their reasons for refusal "were worse than absurd."[219] The board deferred further action until the receipt of the current inspection report which supported Wrigley and Hall. That year construction was started on the *Caledonia*, which made its first successful run to Hazelton in 1891. By April their differences appeared to have been resolved. The board expressed perfect satisfaction with Wrigley's explanations and trusted that he now clearly understood his duties. Henceforth, it would assume responsibility for drafts on London and country advances would fall under Wrigley's jurisdiction.

His reprieve was short-lived. Consistent losses at Bersimis and Saguenay in the Montreal Department had long been a cause for concern and the board concluded that business could not continue without some limitations. In the absence of directives to the contrary, Wrigley chose to reorganize management first and made an exchange of officers at Oxford House and Bersimis. Furious, the board questioned the wisdom and expense of such a move. Its displeasure culminated in a confidential letter from Governor Smith in December 1890 asking for Wrigley's resignation, citing a decision made by the governor and committee the previous September to make certain changes in the administration of the company's affairs which would render necessary Wrigley's retirement. Smith concluded:

> ... the Board have the fullest confidence that so long as it may be necessary you should hold your present office and until relieved in due course you will continue to give the same zealous attention and careful consideration to the discharge of the duties of Commissioner as they have from you throughout your term of service. Let me add that you have the

---

[219]HBCA, D.19/7, fo. 62, Armit to Wrigley, 19 March 1890.

personal best wishes and esteem of myself and every member of the Board.[220]

Wrigley tendered his resignation on 29 December 1890. As a final insult, the board refused to grant his request for an additional year's benefits citing regard for shareholders' interests.[221] Like Chief Commissioner James A. Grahame before him, Wrigley found himself in the position of having to maintain a facade of control when, in fact, he had none.

By the end of 1891 the strain was beginning to take its toll. Wrigley's letters to the commissioned officers became shorter and his tone more brusque. The litany of their offenses grew longer: too many Indian advances at Oxford House, too high prices paid in the Manitoba District, unexplained heavy losses at York Factory, Indian destitution in the Northern and Southern Departments, no accounts received from Lower Fort Garry, the entire outfit damaged in transit from Mackenzie River, unacceptable transportation costs in the Western Department and so on; each letter emphasizing again and again that rules must be adhered to. The number of correspondents declined, and as for the Skeena steamer, which Wrigley had fought for so persistently, the matter was left in T.R. Smith's hands, Wrigley requesting only, "When all is settled, I shall be glad to receive particulars."[222]

To make matters worse, the results from Trading Year '89 were disappointing in all departments. The drop in profits was blamed on widespread destitution among the native population, a low ebb in fur cycles and increased competition despite the large drop in prices experienced at the previous spring sale. As a result, Wrigley dared not recommend the abolition of Indian advances as it would result either in Indians remaining idle around the posts or taking their furs elsewhere.

In a long defence against the board's continued accusations that he had not enforced the rules and "had failed in acquiring a comprehensive grasp of, and a consequent insight into, the administration of the business of the several departments and districts," Wrigley admitted both surprise and concern.[223] When he first came, there was nothing in the commissioner's office, no statements, balance sheets, information or system to help him. A perfect stranger, he had to learn one of the most intricate businesses in existence. Through his systemizing of accounts and statements each sales shop and trading post could now be directly controlled by the commissioner. His many visits to various districts gave him first hand information which was reflected in his

---

[220]HBCA, D.49/3, fos. 497-498, Smith to Wrigley, 10 December 1890.

[221]HBCA, A.6/59, fo. 456, Smith to Wrigley, 21 January 1891.

[222]HBCA, D.14/13, fo. 187, Wrigley to T.R. Smith, 25 November 1890.

[223]HBCA, D.13/10, fo. 258, Wrigley to Armit, 18 February 1891.

comprehensive report of 1888. He concluded, "It is most distasteful to write of myself, but I trust under the circumstances I may be pardoned."[224]

His hopes were in vain as board members hammered away at his choice of officer for Bersimis, which demonstrated to them that business was being conducted in a reckless manner. The entire Montreal Department showed lack of attention as evidenced by diminished profits, escalating Indian balances and ignored tariffs. Despite increased fur returns, the Northern Department was little better and the board's requests for information and explanations escalated.

At the same time, word was quietly being circulated that the trade commissioner's position would soon be vacant and by January 1891 applications were being received.[225] In February Clarence Campbell Chipman began corresponding with board member Thomas Skinner who had advised him of the impending vacancy. Chipman was currently employed with the Canadian Department of Marine and Fisheries and his letters of recommendation were seconded by Sir Charles Tupper, the Canadian High Commissioner in London for whom he had worked as private secretary.[226]

By the end of March 1891, Wrigley advised Governor Smith that he had been warned by his doctor that if he delayed any longer in taking a rest he would suffer serious consequences. In fact, he had already suffered a breakdown and had been forbidden to attend to business.[227] In requesting a six-month leave of absence to restore his health, Wrigley offered to return for a period of six to twelve months if the board so wished. The leave of absence was granted in April but, in a letter to Armit, Governor Smith concluded that it would be of little advantage to have Wrigley return and he was cabled accordingly.

With his dismissal, Wrigley became one more casualty of the board's battle with the balance sheet and of Smith's determination to choose his own staff. Until his general report on the trade was presented in 1888, the board had no comprehensive picture of

---

[224]Ibid.

[225]HBCA, A.10/131, fos. 94-94d, 22 January 1891 and fo. 191, 24 February 1891.

[226]C.C. Chipman (1856-1924) was born and educated in Amherst, Nova Scotia. He began his career with the Canadian civil service in 1876 in the Department of Public Works and later worked in the Finance Department. As private secretary to Sir Charles Tupper, who served as Minister of Railways and Canals in 1883 and the following year as High Commissioner for Canada, he made valuable contacts within government circles. He served on two Commissions to Washington and was accountant for the Canadian section of the Colonial and Indian Exhibition held in London in 1886 in which the Hudson's Bay Company had been involved. By 1891 he was seeking new challenges and he applied for the position of Trade Commissioner (HBCA, A.33/2, fos. 238-242, Chipman to Thomas Skinner, 24 February 1891 and *Who's Who in Western Canada*, vol. 1, p. 138).

[227]HBCA, D.13/10, fo. 333, A. Robertson to Wrigley, 30 March 1891.

the entire operation. It did not like what it saw, and responded by slashing capital investment just when it was needed to hold the line against the competition and dismissing the messenger of its woes.

Although the board considered Wrigley a failure, an assessment of his brief career with the company reveals that he took significant steps towards centralizing management of the fur trade. Through his efforts, a continuous system of inspection was formalized which, for the first time, provided a true picture of each district and post and uncovered areas of waste and mismanagement that had gone undetected for years. Wrigley's reorganization of the traditional system of annual indents and the creation of central depots provided a steady supply of uniformly priced goods at competitive prices while maintaining the quality upon which much of the company's reputation depended.

As fur resources dwindled in the south, Wrigley sought out new areas to tap. Under his leadership, the company established a firm foothold in the fur-rich Cassiar District between Alaska and the Mackenzie River District which was enhanced by the introduction of steamer service on the Skeena River. During his term as trade commissioner, steamers were finally introduced on the Mackenzie River and a new transportation route was developed through Athabaska Landing combining rail, overland and steam transportation to replace the backbreaking Portage la Loche route. This saving of time and money enabled outfits to reach northern destinations the same year that they were shipped from London, cutting travel time in half. Despite the prominence of Donald A. Smith in both the Hudson's Bay Company and the CPR, it was Wrigley who negotiated and maintained the favourable freight rates on which the success of HBC western operations rested.

Another of Wrigley's major accomplishments was convincing the board to follow the competition's lead and update its system of setting tariffs. Previously, tariffs were set on an annual basis after each spring sale. At Wrigley's insistence, the board adopted a system of flexible tariffs which could be updated in response to international market trends. At the same time, the commissioner was allowed some authority to alter them to suit local conditions with which he was more familiar. The adoption of Wrigley's proposal to change the system of posting furs made it possible to determine the actual value of each district and post, providing a better foundation on which to effect change.

Although many positive changes had been made to the company's fur trade operations, its commercial ventures had fallen far short of expectations. Despite costly upgrading, its mills could no longer compete with the numerous small independent operations that were springing up across the prairies. By 1891 three of its five mills had been destroyed by fire and the remainder were to be sold in the unlikely event a buyer could be found.

Hopes for an aggressive retail expansion policy to meet the needs of a population boom had also been dashed. Instead of enjoying the benefits of a prosperous economy, Wrigley was forced to contend with the after-effects of the retail collapse coupled with repercussions from the North West Rebellion. As a result, his tenure was marked less by growth than an attempt to hold the line in the face of a depressed economy, recalcitrant commissioned officers, profit-conscious shareholders and an unenterprising board resistant to change.   Although he could express some satisfaction in the reorganization of the company's buying and supply operations, improvements in sales shop management and small-scale expansion into prairie towns, these actions were, for the most part, reactions to immediate conditions rather than part of a long-term marketing strategy.

Wrigley sailed for England on 12 May 1891, a broken man. The day before his departure from Winnipeg he was honoured at a reception at Government House where, in response to the formal address, he expressed confidence that his health would be restored after a change and rest.[228] Arrangements had been made for Factor William Clark of the Winnipeg Office to take control of the business until Commissioner Chipman's arrival. Clark accepted reluctantly for, as he confided to Roderick MacFarlane, he had "not felt right for a long time and now I am much worse. I can't sleep & am getting a tired sort of way that I have no pleasure in life outside of my own house. I must get away soon or I will ruin my health forever. This new Commissioner business is a most foolish action of the Board at least we all think so. It is an insult to us all..."[229]

With the appointment of Wrigley's successor, the company embarked on the final phase of its transition from a monopolistic fur trade partnership to a diversified corporation. The path had not been an easy one. Lacking past experience on which to draw, the company could only proceed by trial and error. Retention of its trade monopoly would have afforded a welcome cushion, but its surrender was the price paid for the opportunity to diversify into land and general trade. This factor alone would not have been critical if the North West had remained relatively isolated during the transition phase. Once Rupert's Land became part of Canada, however, it had to be secured and this could only be done by the construction of a transcontinental system of transportation. While the railway brought settlers to the west to buy the land and support commercial ventures, it also encouraged competition, ranging from small independent traders to branch outlets of established eastern firms.

As a result, the company was forced to contend with the loss of its monopoly at the same time that it faced major decisions on which direction its interests in fur, land

---

[228]*Winnipeg Tribune*, 14 May 1891. Little is known of Wrigley's private life after his departure. His only personal papers in Canadian repositories for this period are those in the Roderick MacFarlane Collection with whom he corresponded sporadically for two decades. He seldom saw any company men with the exception of Donald A. Smith from time to time and brief visits from William Clark and his family. The only official news he received came from annual reports and meetings he attended as a shareholder (NAC, *MacFarlane Papers*, Wrigley to MacFarlane, 1 July 1902). He was under a doctor's care for much of the time and admitted in 1908 that "since my return from Canada I have not been allowed to take up any definite or public work" (ibid., 6 April 1908). He died 20 February 1926, at age 87, at his London home at Kensington Park Gardens and was buried in Kensal Green Cemetery (*The Times*, 22 February 1926).

[229]NAC, *MacFarlane Papers*, fo. 1419, Clark to MacFarlane, 29 May 1891.

and retail trade should take. Each of the three had its proponents, the most vocal of these being company shareholders whose expectations in the area of land development were totally at variance with the realities of the Canadian west. There was little time to reflect and weigh the consequences, however, for once an opportunity was lost to more aggressive entrepreneurs, it could rarely be regained.

The dominant theme of the post-1870 period in the company's history was the formation of a more centralized administrative structure and, under Wrigley's direction, this program was accelerated. His first act, the establishment of a uniform system of inspection, provided a basis on which to make recommendations for change. To complement this, annual reports from the various districts were revived, in an attempt to bring autonomous departments under the jurisdiction of the trade commissioner. Reforms were not accomplished easily as department heads fought, often successfully, against any challenge to their authority, but a realignment of the North American corporate structure was essential to the company's intent, and slowly but surely definite progress was made.

In the past, the primary source of information available to the board had been the year-end accounting which was based on an inventory of assets and the results of shipments made to England. Since accounting procedures at the department level were primitive, there were no means of preparing an accurate profit and loss statement or of making a detailed comparison between outfits. Wrigley's improved systems of accounting and evaluating furs enabled the company to determine for the first time the actual rather than apparent value of individual posts and districts. At the same time, his success in persuading the board to adopt a more flexible tariff system that could be updated periodically in response to market fluctuations finally brought the Canadian hinterland into closer contact with international markets. Such reform would have been impossible without improved systems of communications which finally dispelled the isolation that had allowed many of the commissioned officers to work in a semi-autonomous manner.

The company's efforts to consolidate control would not be without casualties. Despite Wrigley's constant concern that the commissioned officers be treated with consideration, their inability to adapt was a recurring theme in his annual reports as he struggled to keep the company's mills and sales shops afloat. Officers traditionally enjoyed positions of power and prestige within the company and the community at large and, as profit-sharing partners, they were a vital element in the trading operations. In the past, they had successfully used the threat of mass resignation to gain financial concessions, most notably through the formation of the Fur Trade Party in 1879. Declining fur trade profits, uncertainty about the annual guarantee and alterations to their supply tariffs made by the board without prior consultation fuelled concerns for the future which led to their demands for a pension plan.

The board's attempt to discredit their claims, through the dismissal of their self-appointed spokesman Roderick MacFarlane, met with defeat, as Wrigley had warned, but in the end the board turned it to advantage. Although MacFarlane's reinstatement and the inauguration of a pension plan appeared, at first, to be a major victory for the commissioned officers, the pension plan gave the board a legitimate excuse to rid itself of senior officers who had the most claims and opened the way for younger men with commercial experience. Lists of retirees were drawn up by the trade commissioner and the board and those designated were expected to submit their application voluntarily or suffer enforced retirement. Under the terms of the Deed Poll, pensions were granted strictly at the board's pleasure and a restriction clause ensured that recipients could not go into opposition, effectively destroying the leverage that had been wielded so successfully in the past.

Another blow occurred at the 1887 Council when it was announced that henceforth no new commissions would be granted to men who had entered the service after 1870. With this decision, it was simply a matter of time until the company became a completely salaried operation. The elimination of commissioned ranks within the company was finally accomplished in 1893 when the rights of the Deed Poll of 1871 were acquired by the board in return for guaranteed salaries.

It did not take long for the officers to realize that the collective powers that had enabled them to gain concessions in the past were evaporating. When MacFarlane approached Chief Factor Alex Munro in 1890 to demand pension rights for the families of the late Chief Factors Richard Hardisty, Lawrence Clarke and James Cotter, Munro advised him that the new board under Smith would not likely look favourably on his request. He cautioned against any further action: "Fortunately, in the good old times, the officers could feel secure, holding in their own hand very substantial powers & a protest from them wd command respect. But circs are very different now, as you well know."[230]

Frustrated and feeling betrayed, many officers viewed Wrigley as the instrument of injustice and greeted his resignation with approval. Factor Donald C. McTavish wrote:

> Wrigley got his reward in the end, he is leaving hated and abused on all sides he acted a mean selfish part; looked down upon the Fur Traders and did his best to please the Board. He had to leave; has not got one friend at home [England] & Sir Donald would hardly speak to him, ... The Council was a farce, he could not do or say anything, he should have remained at home.[231]

Others were more charitable. J. Odgen Grahame, son and secretary of former chief commissioner James A. Grahame, blamed Wrigley's advisers for his failure to make the business pay[232] and William Clark, who worked with Wrigley in the Winnipeg office, staunchly defended him against all critics.

---

[230]NAC, *MacFarlane Papers*, Munro to MacFarlane, 13 December 1890.

[231]Ibid., fo. 1396, McTavish to MacFarlane, 28 March 1891.

[232]Ibid., fo. 1416, Grahame to MacFarlane, 21 May 1891.

In retrospect, although the officers' appraisal of Wrigley was unfairly harsh, their uneasy relationship with him could not have been otherwise. Given the limited opportunity for personal contact, the officers' natural mistrust of an English outsider and Wrigley's own personal reticence, which was often misconstrued as aloofness, it was impossible for most officers to gain any true impression of the man behind the title of trade commissioner.[233] In their minds the person and the title were one and, as the person ultimately responsible to the board and who represented the board to them, Wrigley was perceived to be unsympathetic to their concerns.

For his part, Wrigley made every effort to treat the officers with tact and consideration. In the only public conflict between the board and its officers, which followed the dismissal of MacFarlane, Wrigley interceded on the latter's behalf at many officers' request and added his own personal appeal which won MacFarlane his subsequent reinstatement. Confidential efforts on behalf of other disgraced officers remained unknown to all but the board.

In contrast to the company's fur trade and transportation operations, relatively few innovations were made in the area of general trade. Costly expansion was curtailed in favour of upgrading older establishments, placing others on a more permanent footing and, in a final admission of defeat, phasing out the milling operations. In his General Report Wrigley questioned whether the company would be wiser to concentrate retail efforts in urban and more settled rural areas instead of spreading itself across the sparsely settled prairies.[234] In committing itself to retail trade, the company faced the challenge of trying to be all things to all people, from affluent urban shoppers to northern natives. At the same time it was forced to compete with specialty shops and aggressive independent traders for increasingly scarce dollars. Wrigley's reluctance to take advantage of new opportunities in advertising placed the company at further disadvantage and only strengthened its elitist reputation. On the rare occasion when a major competitor such as I.G. Baker & Son was bought out, any advantage gained was short-lived as profits from government contracts dwindled and other competitors stepped in.

What held many of the HBC's customers was its reputation for quality which it could not afford to compromise but which failed to attract working-class trade. Despite these obstacles, however, Wrigley was successful in introducing more formal procedures for the operation of the sales shops, including the bonding of clerks, as well as improvements in accounting procedures and the purchase and supply of goods.

---

[233]Unlike his counterpart, Land Commissioner Brydges, Wrigley was a very private person who kept a relatively low profile within the business community and Winnipeg society. There are very few objective references to him, but the ones that exist remark on his courtesy and gentlemanly qualities. See particularly Franklin Remington, "Harvard to York Factory in 1888", p. 9.

[234]This step was taken almost a century later with the sale of the Hudson's Bay Company's Northern Stores Department in 1987.

With Wrigley's dismissal in 1891 the company turned away from the two-tiered system of middle management which it had introduced in 1874. After one year as trade commissioner, Clarence C. Chipman was appointed to the joint post of commissioner and land commissioner, head of the entire Canadian operation, the same position that Charles Brydges was to have assumed but never did.

A constant factor in the company's post-1870 personnel changes was Donald A. Smith. It is unfortunate that there has been no major study of the man since Beckles Willson's hagiographic biography was published in 1915, a year after Smith's death. Primary sources reveal that he was respected by many commissioned officers for his long years in the service as well as his investment skills and they used his influence within the company and public circles to represent their demands to the board on several occasions. But he was also difficult to work with, resented the ideas of his colleagues and was "a great hater".[235] Frequent clashes with James A. Grahame and the latter's appointment to replace Smith in the position chief commissioner earned him Smith's ill-will and it was Smith's insistence on an enquiry into alleged wrongdoing in the land department that resulted in Grahame's dismissal. Charles Brydges, Smith's successor in the land department, was no more fortunate and after constant harassment by Smith, died of a heart attack as he was being hounded from office.

Wrigley's relationship with Smith followed a somewhat similar course. He was never considered "Smith's man" as Chipman would be.[236] Unlike Brydges and Chipman, he did not have well-placed contacts in the Canadian government or the company, or within the ranks of the commissioned officers as Grahame had. This was not a problem during Wrigley's early years when Smith, as senior member of the Canadian subcommittee, was concentrating on Brydges and the land department and Wrigley's credentials had been firmly established by his administration of the supply system during the North West Rebellion. But when it became obvious that Wrigley could not translate the aspirations of management and especially the shareholders into reality, he had nowhere to turn for support. What had protected him was the fact that the board had no real perception of how the company was actually doing other than from annual reports. Although the subcommittee kept close watch on the operations of the land department, it did little more than approve indents for the fur trade department and its early relations with Wrigley were cordial.

In presenting his report on the company's trading operations to the board in 1888, however, Wrigley sealed his own fate. His innovations in inspection systems, indenting and accounting procedures resulted in the most accurate picture the company had ever received of its affairs and it was a bleak one.

Although the board placed the bulk of the blame on Wrigley's inability to put its trade operations on a more profitable basis, the Canadian subcommittee should have been

---

[235]E.M. Wrong, "Donald Alexander Smith" in *Dictionary of National Biography 1912-1921*, p. 498.

[236]Inkyo, *Reflections of Inkyo on the Great Company*, p. 498.

an equally vulnerable target, given its mandate to "supervise the affairs of the Company in North America".[237] As the senior member of the two-man committee Smith naturally should have been called to account. Luck and timing were on Smith's side, however. The same month that Wrigley presented his report to the board, Smith was elected to succeed Deputy Governor John Rose and was elevated shortly thereafter in 1889 to the governorship.

As governor, Smith immediately set out to put his personal stamp upon the company's management. Land Commissioner Brydges was only the first casualty. Officers' overdrafts, the Skeena steamer controversy and staffing problems in the Montreal Department provided sufficient ammunition for Governor Smith to demand Wrigley's resignation the following year. Several other departures followed. In April 1891 the company's secretary, William Armit, resigned after 31 years of service under seven governors, citing ill health.[238] Factor James Lawson applied to retire as land agent in order to accept a position as manager of a general mercantile business in Victoria.[239] The Western Department was further weakened that year by the retirement of Chief Factor Alex Munro, one of the spokesmen for the commissioned officers in their demands for a pension,[240] and Assistant Commissioner T.R. Smith.

With the complete restructuring of middle management, it was doubtless hoped that fresh insights could be applied to old problems. A more fundamental change in corporate policy was needed at the board level, however, if the company was to thrive. Although the selection of men from outside the company's ranks to head its Canadian operations could be regarded as an attempt on the part of the board to separate the policy-setting responsibilities of ownership from that of its professional managers, who would henceforth be responsible for operational control, it failed to follow through.[241] Throughout his term of office, Wrigley's attempts to revitalize the trade were consistently hampered by a board resistant to change and swayed by short-term financial considerations. This, combined with an unrelenting economic depression, presented overwhelming odds in the face of which Wrigley's downfall was inevitable.

Although he had managed to accomplish much, in the end it mattered little if he could not maintain the confidence of the board, on one hand, and the commissioned

---

[237]HBCA, A.6/55, fos. 302-306, Armit to Brydges and Grahame, 5 May 1884.

[238]HBCA, A.10/131, fo. 338, Armit to the governor and committee, 6 April 1891 and A.10/82A, fo. 114, Armit to Donald A. Smith, 31 October 1891.

[239]Ibid., fo. 82, Lawson to Donald A. Smith, 20 July 1891.

[240]When Munro refused the position of Land Commissioner in 1889, Smith expressed his disappointment to Armit, noting "it is doubtless well that his [Munro's] resignation as on the 1st June ensuing should be accepted" (HBCA, A.12/53, Smith to Armit, 22 February 1889).

[241] J.E. Rea, "Introduction", p. xxi-xxii.

officers, on the other. The latter was crucial for without their support, as well as that of the board, Wrigley was left powerless when the final accounting came. But neither Wrigley nor the service had failed the company: its leadership had proved ill-prepared to define a new future.

BIBLIOGRAPHY

UNPUBLISHED SOURCES

ARCHIVAL

Glenbow-Alberta Institute, Calgary.
Richard Charles Hardisty Papers, 1845-1958.

Historical Society of Montana, Helena.
Papers relating to I.G. Baker.

Hudson's Bay Company Archives, Provincial Archives of Manitoba,
Winnipeg, Manitoba

<u>Section A London Records</u>

A.1/152-154	Minute Book	1882-1892
A.1/182-188	Sub Committee Minutes	1882-1890
A.4/47	London Agenda Book	1881-1884
A.4/49	do.	1889-1891
A.5/52	London Correspondence Outwards - General	1883-1885
A.5/57	do.	1888-1889
A.5/59	do.	1890-1891
A.6/55-59	London Correspondence Book Outwards - HBC Official	1883-1891
A.7/4,5	London Locked Private Letter Book	1863-1875
		1880-1921
A.10/82A	Donald A. Smith - Inward and Outward Correspondence 1889-1904	
A.10/84	London Inward Correspondence General	Jul-Dec 1871
A.10/112	do.	May-Aug 1882
A.10/115-117	do.	Oct 1883-Aug 1884
A.10/127	do.	Jan-Jun 1889
A.10/130,131	do.	Jul 1890-Jun 1891
A.11/100	London Inward Correspondence from HBC Posts - Winnipeg	1871-1873
A.12/31-33	London Inward Correspondence from Commissioners - Joseph Wrigley	1890-1891
A.12/47	London Inward Correspondence from Commissioners - James A. Grahame	1879
A.12/53	London Inward Correspondence from Donald A. Smith and Canadian Sub Committee	1884-1897
A.33/1	Agreement between Governor and Committee and Commissioned Officers - Revocation of Deed Poll of 1834	1871-1872
A.33/2	Commissioned Officers Indentures and Agreements A-C	

A.33/3	Commissioned Officers Indentures and Agreements D-L	
A.33/5	Commissioned Officers Indentures and Agreements N-Z	
A.37/19	Deed of Surrender	19 Nov 1869
A.37/20	Drafts of Deed Poll of 1871	1871-1887

Original HBC Deed Poll for Conducting
the Trade in North America and for
defining the rights and prescribing the
duties of officers dated 19 December 1871.

Section D

D.13/6-11	Commissioner's Outward Letterbook - London	1882-1891
D.14/8-13	Commissioners Outward Letterbook - to HBC Officials	1884-1891
D.15/3-5	Commissioner's Outward Letterbook - General	1881-1889
D.16/2	Commissioner's Private & Confidential Letterbook	1887-1893
D.17/1-2	Commissioner's Outward Letterbook - Canadian Sub Committee and later to the HBC Governor (Donald A. Smith)	1884-1894
D.18/12	Copies of Commissioner's Outward Telegrams to London	1889-1893
D.18/13	Copies of Commissioner's Outward Outward Telegrams to Sir Donald A. Smith	1889-1892
D.19/12-17	Commissioner's Inward Correspondence - London	1885-1890
D.20/23/2	Commissioner's Inward Correspondence - General	June 1882
D.24/1	Standing Rules and Regulations, revised, October 1877	
D.26/12	Papers relating to the Hudson's Bay Company mills	1879-1889
D.26/32	Pension Schemes from Assorted Businesses and Government Agencies	1880-1903
D.38/4	Minute Book of Meetings of the Northern Department	1880-1884
D.38/6	Minutes of Meetings of the Montreal Department	1875-1890
D.38/8	Commissioner's Draft of HBC Rules and Regulations	1887
D.38/9	Annual Meetings' Minutes, Motion Papers and Drafts Concerning HBC Rules and Regulations	1887
D.48/1-45	Canadian Sub Committee Inward Correspondence	May 1884-Oct 1891
D.49/1, 2	Canadian Sub Committee Correspondence	1884-1892
D.49/3	D.A. Smith's Correspondence with Company Servants written from London and Letters to Armit from Smith	1890-1893
D.50/1, 2	Canadian Sub Committee	1884-1886

Section E
E.9/3   Letters and Telegrams - North West Rebellion   1885-1886
E.9/4   Account Book - North West Rebellion   1885
E.9/28   Declarations and Statements re Losses caused by   1885-1888
                  the North West Rebellion
E.9/30   Winnipeg, Northern Department and Commissioner's
                  Office Correspondence and working papers relating to claims
E.21/4   Joseph James Hargrave - Correspondence   1885-1888
E.38/3   Chief Factor James Mcdougall Papers.   24 May -
                  Journal of inspection from Winnipeg   14 Nov 1990
                  to New Caledonia District
E.39/3   Archibald McDonald Papers   1858-1894
E.40/1   Dr. Robert Bell Correspondence Inward   1878-1899

Section F
F.36/1   Winnipeg and Western Transportation Company -   1878-1900
                  Minute Book
F.48/1   Red River and Assiniboine Bridge Company Minutes   1880-1909

RG Series
RG3 Series 43   Memorandums on the Fur Trade Commissions   1934

Hudson's Bay Company Library, Hudson's Bay Company, Winnipeg.
    Piers, Sir Charles. "Past and Present Transportation Systems of the
    Hudson's Bay Company with Routes, Voyages and Journeys."
    Unpublished manuscript, 1926.

Legislative Library of Manitoba, Winnipeg.
    Biographical Scrapbook 1.

Metropolitan Toronto Library.
    Alexander Matheson Papers.

National Archives of Canada, Ottawa.
    Canadian Pacific Railway Papers. Van Horne letterbooks
        (microfilm).
    J.P.R.A. Caron Papers.
    Edgar Dewdney Papers (microfilm).
    Sandford Fleming Papers.

Roderick MacFarlane Papers.
Sir Gilbert John Elliot Minto, fourth earl of (Lord
  Melgund). Papers (microfilm).
North West Navigation Company Limited. Daily Journal
  of Colvile and Princess steamers, 1885.
Records of the Department of the Interior regarding the
  North West Rebellion Losses Claims.

National Library of Canada, Ottawa.
Papers relating to the Hudson's Bay Company, 1882-1883.

Provincial Archives of British Columbia, Victoria.
French, Olive, Leta French and T.W. Hall (eds.). "Autobiography
  of Charles H. French, 1867-1940." Unpublished manuscript.

Provincial Archives of Manitoba, Winnipeg.
Anonymous. "Memorandum respecting the position of the Commissioned
  Officers of the Fur Trade in relation to the H.B.C. under the
  Deed Poll 1821-1892 together with some N.W.C. and other connective notes."
  c. 1910.

UNPUBLISHED MANUSCRIPTS, THESES, AND DISSERTATIONS
Baril, Evelyn. "The Hudson's Bay Company and the Urbanization of the Prairies, 1870
  to 1888." Unpublished manuscript, University of Winnipeg, 1977.

Bellan, Reuben C. "The Development of Winnipeg as a Metropolitan Centre." Ph.D.
  dissertation, Columbia University, 1958.

Bonar, James C. *Canadian Pacific Railway Company and its Contributions Towards the
  Early Development and to the Continued Progress of Canada.* Vol. 5. Unpublished
  manuscript, 1950.

Dyck, Noel Evan. "The Administration of Federal Indian Aid in the North-West
  Territories, 1879-1885." M.A. thesis, University of Saskatchewan, 1970.

Francis, James M. "Business, Enterprise, and the National Policy: the Role of T.C.
  Power & Brother and I.G. Baker & Company in the Political and Economic
  Development of the Southwestern Canadian Prairies and Northern Montana, 1870-
  1893." M.A. thesis, University of British Columbia, 1978.

Kemp, Herbert Douglas. "The Department of the Interior in the West 1873-1883." M.A. thesis, University of Manitoba, 1950.

Nigol, Paul. "Efficiency and Economy: Commissioner C.C. Chipman and the Hudson's Bay Company, 1891 - 1911." M.A. thesis, University of Manitoba, 1994.

Oleson, Robert V. "The Commissioned Officers of the Hudson's Bay Company and the Deed Poll in the 1870's with Particular Emphasis on the Fur Trade Party, 1878-1879." M.A. thesis, University of Manitoba, 1977.

Ray A.J. "Marketing Canadian Furs, 1870-1945: A Preliminary Discussion." Unpublished manuscript, 1985.

Richtik, James M. "Manitoba Settlement: 1870 to 1886." Ph.D. dissertation, University of Manitoba, 1971.

Rostecki, Randolph R. "The Growth of Winnipeg, 1870-1886." M.A. thesis, University of Manitoba, 1980.

Sealey, Gary David. "History of the Hudson's Bay Company 1870-1900." M.A. thesis, University of Western Ontario, 1969.

Simpson, G. Howard D. "The Sales Organization of the Fur Trade." Commerce undergraduate thesis, University of Toronto, 1925.

Stardom, Eleanor. "Adapting to Altered Circumstances: Trade Commissioner Joseph Wrigley and the Hudson's Bay Company, 1884-1891." M.A. thesis, University of Manitoba, 1987.

Tway, Duane Converse. "The Influence of the Hudson's Bay Company Upon Canada, 1870-1889." Ph.D. dissertation, University of California, 1962.

PRIVATE HOLDINGS

Correspondence between Eleanor Stardom and Dr. Joseph Wrigley (grandson), 1984.

Correspondence between Eleanor Stardom and Mrs. Jo Merry (great-granddaughter), 1984.

PUBLISHED SOURCES

NEWSPAPERS
The Commercial (Winnipeg), 1886-1888.
Daily British Colonist (Victoria), 1885.
The Daily Colonist (Victoria), 1884, 1891.
Edmonton Bulletin, 1887.
The Huddersfield Examiner, 1874.
Manitoba Free Press, 1885, 1891, 1929.
The Manitoba Sun, 1887.
The Province (Vancouver), 1958.
The Times (London), 1926.
Victoria Daily Colonist, 1887, 1890, 1905, 1948, 1951.
Victoria Daily Times, 1920.
Vancouver Daily World, 1891.
Winnipeg Daily Times, 1885, 1891.
Winnipeg Tribune, 1891.

BOOKS AND ARTICLES
Alcock, F.J. "Past and Present Trade Routes to the Canadian Northwest." *Geographical Review*. Vol. 10. August 1920: 57-83.

Anonymous. *The Riel Rebellion, 1885*. Montreal: Witness Printing House, 1885.

Artibise, Alan F.J. *Winnipeg, A Social History of Urban Growth 1874-1914*. Montreal: McGill-Queen's University Press, 1975.

_____. *Winnipeg, An Illustrated History*. Toronto: James Lorimer & Company, 1977.

Beal, Bob and Rod Macleod. *Prairie Fire, the 1885 North-West Rebellion*. Edmonton: Hurtig Publishers, 1984.

Begg, Alexander. *History of the North-West*. Vol. 2. Toronto: Hunter, Rose & Company, 1894.

Bliss, Michael. *Northern Enterprise: Five Centuries of Canadian Business*. Toronto: McClelland and Stewart, 1987.

Boulton, C.A. *Reminiscences of the North-West Rebellions*. Toronto: Grip Printing and Publishing Co., 1886.

Bowsfield, Hartwell (ed.). *The Letters of Charles John Brydges, 1879-1882, Hudson's Bay Company Land Commissioner.* Winnipeg: Hudson's Bay Record Society, 1977.

_____. *The Letters of Charles John Brydges 1883-1889, Hudson's Bay Company Land Commissioner.* Winnipeg: Hudson's Bay Record Society, 1981.

Brown, J. "H.B.C. Officers Once Controlled a Northern Empire." *The Beaver,* December 1921: 2-8.

_____. "The 'Lords of the North' in Annual Conclave." *The Beaver,* July 1921: 2-6.

Bryce, George. *The Remarkable History of the Hudson's Bay Company Including that of the French Traders of North-Western Canada and of the North-West, XY, and Astor Fur Companies.* Toronto: William Briggs, 1900.

Camsell, Charles. *Son of the North.* Toronto: Ryerson Press, 1954.

Canada. House of Commons, *Debates,* 1885.

_____. *Sessional Papers,* 1884-1891.

Chandler, Alfred D. Jr. *The Visible Hand: The Managerial Revolution in American Business.* Cambridge: Belknap Press, 1977.

Comfort, Darlene J. *Ribbon of Water and Steamboats North.* Fort McMurray: Comfort Enterprises, 1974.

den Otter, A.A. "The Hudson's Bay Company's Prairie Transportation Problem 1870-85." In John E. Foster (ed.), *The Developing West, Essays on Canadian History in Honour of Lewis H. Thomas.* Edmonton: University of Alberta Press, 1983.

Department of Militia and Defence of the Dominion of Canada. *Report of Lieutenant-Colonel W.H. Jackson on Matters in Connection with the Suppression of the Rebellion in the North-West Territories, in 1885.* Ottawa: MacLean, Roger & Co., 1887.

Elliot, Hon. Arthur D. *The Life of George Joachim Goschen, First Viscount Goschen 1831-1907.* Vol. 1. London: Longmans, Green and Co., 1911.

Fleming, Sandford. *Observations by Mr. Sandford Fleming on the General Land Policy of the Hudson's Bay Company.* London: Sir Joseph Causton & Sons, 1882.

Galbraith, John S. "Land Policies of the Hudson's Bay Company, 1870-1913." *Canadian Historical Review.* Vol. 32, March 1951: 1-21.

Goldring, Philip. *Papers on the Labour System of the Hudson's Bay Company 1821-1900*. Vol. 1. Manuscript Report No. 362. Vol. 2. Manuscript Report No. 412. Ottawa: Parks Canada, 1979, 1980.

Gordon, Stanley. "Lawrence Clarke." In *Dictionary of Canadian Biography*. Vol. XI. Toronto: University of Toronto Press, 1982.

Hudson's Bay Company. *Charters, Statutes, Orders In Council, etc. Relating to the Hudson's Bay Company*. London: Hudson's Bay Company, 1931.

_____. *Deed Poll by the Governor and Company of Hudson's Bay for Conducting their Trade in North America and for Defining the Rights and Prescribing the Duties of their Offices*. London: Sir Joseph Causton & Sons, 1871.

_____. *Hudson's Bay Company, A Brief History*. London: Hudson's Bay House, 1934.

_____. *Proceedings at a General Court of the Governor and Company of Adventurers of England Trading into Hudson's Bay*. London: Sir Joseph Causton & Sons, 1870-1891.

_____. *Report by the Secretary on the Company's Trade*. London: Sir Joseph Causton & Sons, 1882.

_____. *Report of the Governor and Committee of the Hudson's Bay Company, to be Laid Before the Shareholders*. London: Sir Joseph Causton & Sons, 1870-1891.

Inkyo. *Reflections of Inkyo on the Great Company*. London: London General Press, 1931.

Innis, Harold A. *The Fur Trade in Canada*. Toronto: University of Toronto Press, 1956.

Kerr, Donald. "Wholesale Trade on the Canadian Plains." In Howard Palmer, *The Settlement of the West*. Calgary: University of Calgary, 1977.

Kingston, W.H.G. *Snow-Shoes and Canoes; or, The Early Days of a Fur Trader in the Hudson's Bay Territory*. London: Sampson Low, Marston, Searle, & Revington, 1887.

Klassen, Henry C. "The Hudson's Bay Company in Southwestern Alberta, 1874-1905." In Jennifer S.H. Brown, W.J. Eccles and Donald P. Heldman (eds.), *The Fur Trade Revisited*. East Lansing: Michigan State University Press, 1994.

Klassen, Henry C. "I.G. Baker & Co. in Calgary, 1875-1884." *Montana, The Magazine of Western History*, Summer 1985: 40-54.

Large, R. Geddes. *The Skeena, River of Destiny*. Vancouver: Mitchell Press, 1957.

Laurie, Major General. *Report of Major General Laurie, Commanding Base and Lines of Communication, upon matters in connection with the suppression of the Rebellion in the North-West Territories in 1885*. Ottawa: MacLean, Roger & Co., 1887.

Lockyer, H.T. "The Rise of H.B.C. Vancouver Retail Establishment." *The Beaver*, December 1920: 20-22.

MacGregor, J.G. *Paddle Wheels to Bucket-Wheels on the Athabaska*. Toronto: McClelland and Stewart, 1974.

MacKay, Douglas. *The Honourable Company. A History of the Hudson's Bay Company*. Toronto: McClelland and Stewart, 1949.

Malcomson, Robert. "Northcote: Paddlewheels and Glory on the Saskatchewan." *The Beaver*, August/September 1993: 4-9.

Martin, Chester. *Dominion Lands Policy*. Toronto: McClelland and Stewart Limited, 1973.

_____. *The Natural Resources Question, The Historical Basis of Provincial Claims*. Winnipeg: King's Printer, 1920.

McCullough, A.B. *Papers Relating to the North-West Mounted Police and Fort Walsh*. Manuscript Report No. 213. Ottawa: Parks Canada, 1977.

_____. *Prices, Transportation Costs and Supply Patterns in Western Canada, 1873-1885*. Microfiche Report Series No. 78. Ottawa: Parks Canada, 1982.

McKenzie, N.M.W.J. *The Men of the Hudson's Bay Company*. Fort William: Times Journal Presses, 1921.

McLeod, Margaret Arnett. "The Company in Winnipeg." *The Beaver*, September 1940: 6-11.

McTavish, George Simpson. *Behind the Palisades*. Sidney: Gray's Publishing Canada, 1963.

Mitchell, Elaine Allan. "Edward Watkin and the Buying-Out of the Hudson's Bay Company." *Canadian Historical Review*. Vol. 34, September 1953: 219-244.

Morse, Eric W. *Canoe Routes of the Voyageurs, The Geography and Logistics of the Canadian Fur Trade.* Toronto: Quetico Foundation, 1962.

Morton, Arthur S. *History of Prairie Settlement.* Toronto: Macmillan Company of Canada, 1938.

Morton, Desmond and Reginald H. Roy. *Telegrams of the North-West Campaign 1885.* Toronto: Champlain Society, 1972.

Parker, C.W. (ed.). *Who's Who in Western Canada.* Vol. 1. Vancouver: Canadian Press Association, Limited, 1911.

Peel, Bruce. *Steamboats on the Saskatchewan.* Saskatoon: Western Producer, 1972.

Poland, Henry. *Fur Bearing Animals In Nature and In Commerce.* London: Gurney & Jackson, 1892.

Prest, J. "From Pioneer Trading Post to Great Department Store." *The Beaver*, March 1921: 2-6.

Ray, A.J. *The Canadian Fur Trade in the Industrial Age.* Toronto: University of Toronto Press, 1990.

_____. "The Decline of Paternalism in the Hudson's Bay Company Fur Trade, 1870-1945." In Rosemary E. Ommer (ed.) *Merchant Credit and Labour Strategies in Historical Perspective.* Fredericton: Acadiensis Press, 1990.

_____. "York Factory, The Crisis of Transition, 1870-1880." *The Beaver*, Autumn 1982: 26-31.

Rea, J.E. "The Hudson's Bay Company and the North-West Rebellion." *The Beaver*, Summer 1982: 43-57.

Rea, Kenneth J. *The Political Economy of the Canadian North, An Interpretation of the Course of Development in the Northern Territories of Canada to the Early 1960s.* Toronto: University of Toronto Press.

Remington, Franklin. "Harvard to York Factory in 1888." *The Beaver*, December 1944: 8-12.

Rich, E.E. *Hudson's Bay Company 1670-1870.* Vol. 3. 1821-1870. Toronto: McClelland and Stewart, 1960.

Robert, Rudolph. *Chartered Companies and their Role in the Development of Overseas Trade*. London: G. Bell and Sons, 1969.

Sachs, John C. *Furs and the Fur Trade*. London: Sir Isaac Pitman & Sons, 1923.

Schooling, Sir William. *The Hudson's Bay Company 1670-1920*. London: Hudson's Bay Company, 1920.

Selwood, H. John. "Mr. Brydges' Bridges." *The Beaver*, Summer 1981: 14-22.

Selwood, H. John, and Evelyn Baril. "The Hudson's Bay Company and Prairie Town Development, 1870-1888." In Alan F.J. Artibise (ed.), *Town and City, Aspects of Western Canadian Urban Development*. Regina: Canadian Plains Research Centre, 1981.

Sharp, Paul F. *Whoop-Up Country*. The Canadian American West 1865-1885. Minneapolis: University of Minnesota Press, 1955.

Smith, Shirlee A. "'A Desire to Worry Me Out', Donald Smith's Harassment of Charles Brydges, 1879 - 1889." *The Beaver*, December 1987: 4-11.

_____. "Richard Hardisty." In *Dictionary of Canadian Biography*. Vol. XI. Toronto: University of Toronto Press, 1982.

Stanley, George F.G. *The Birth of Western Canada, A History of the Riel Rebellions*. Toronto: University of Toronto Press, 1963.

_____. "The Fur Trade Party, Part 2." *The Beaver*, December 1953: 21-25.

Stardom, Eleanor. "Twilight of the Fur Trade." *The Beaver*, August/September 1991: 6-18.

Steen & Boyce. *Winnipeg, Manitoba and her Industries*. Winnipeg: Steen & Boyce, 1882.

Tharp, Louise Hall. *Company of Adventurers*. Boston: Little, Brown and Company, 1947.

Tyman, John Langton. *By Section, Township and Range, Studies in Prairie Settlement*. Brandon: Assiniboine Historical Society, 1972.

Walden, Keith. "Speaking Modern: Language, Culture, and Hegemony in Grocery Window Displays, 1887-1920." *Canadian Historical Review*, September, 1989: 285-310

Weeks, Charles. "First H.B.C. Store in Vancouver." *The Beaver*, March 1927: 57.

Willson, Beckles. *Lord Strathcona, The Story of His Life*. London: Methuen & Co., 1902.

_____. *The Life of Lord Strathcona & Mount Royal*. London: Cassell and Company, 1915.

Wilson, Alan, "In A Business Way: C.J. Brydges and the Hudson's Bay Company, 1879-1889." In Carl Berger and Ramsay Cook (eds.), *The West and the Nation, Essays in Honour of W.L. Morton*. Toronto: McClelland and Stewart, 1976.

Wrigley, Joseph. *Report of the Commissioner to the Governor, Deputy Governor and Committee of the Hudson's Bay Company of the Trade of the Company*. n.p., 188

Wrong, E.M. "Donald Alexander Smith." In *Dictionary of National Biography 1912-1921*. London: Oxford University Press, 1927.

Zaslow, Morris. *The Opening of the Canadian North 1870-1914*. Toronto: McClelland and Stewart, 1971.

INDEX

DATE DUE